My Hope Is Built ...:
Christian Perspectives on Decisions at the End of Life

My Hope Is Built...:

Christian Perspectives on Decisions at the End of Life

F. Walton Avery, MD, MTS

iUniverse, Inc.
Bloomington

My Hope Is Built …:
Christian Perspectives on Decisions at the End of Life

iUniverse books may be ordered through booksellers or by contacting:

iUniverse
1663 Liberty Drive
Bloomington, IN 47403
www.iuniverse.com
1-800-Authors (1-800-288-4677)

Because of the dynamic nature of the Internet, any web addresses or links contained in this book may have changed since publication and may no longer be valid. The views expressed in this work are solely those of the author and do not necessarily reflect the views of the publisher, and the publisher hereby disclaims any responsibility for them.

Any people depicted in stock imagery provided by Thinkstock are models, and such images are being used for illustrative purposes only.

Certain stock imagery © Thinkstock.

ISBN: 978-1-4620-6413-7 (sc)
ISBN: 978-1-4620-6415-1 (hc)
ISBN: 978-1-4620-6414-4 (e)

Printed in the United States of America

iUniverse rev. date: 11/28/2011

For my wife, Laura, and my three children,
Chase, Christian and Claire.

My Hope Is Built …: Christian Perspectives on Decisions at the End of Life

"My hope is built on nothing less than Jesus' blood and righteousness."[1]

"Jesus keep me near the cross there a Precious fountain free to all, a healing stream, flows from Calv'ry's mountain"[2]

"That oath (Hippocratic) never felt safe to me, hanging around my neck with the stethoscope, not for a minute. I could not accept the contract: that every child born human upon the earth comes with a guarantee of perfect health and old age clutched in its small fist."[3]

"The wise man (person) looks at death with honesty, dignity, and calm, recognizing that the tragedy it brings is inherent in the great gift of life."[4]

"O Israel, hope in the Lord! For with the Lord there is steadfast love, and with him is great power to redeem."[5]

"There is a balm in Gilead to make the wounded whole…"[6]

"Hope is the thing left to us in a bad time."[7]

---

1   "My Hope is Built": *The United Methodist Hymnal* (Nashville: The United Methodist Publishing House, 1993), p.368.

2   "Near the Cross": *The Hymnal for Worship and Celebration* (Waco, Texas: Word Music, 1936), p.385.

3   Kingsolver, B.: *The Poisonwood Bible* (New York: HarperPerennial, 1998), p.528.

4   Corliss L.: *The Philosophy of Humanism* (New York: Frederick Unger, 1982).

5   Ps.130:7, NRSV.

6   "There is a Balm in Gilead": *The Hymnal 1982* (New York: The Church Hymnal Corporation, 1985), p. 676.

7   Irish Proverb.

TABLE OF CONTENTS

PROLOGUE

In the context of the Christian faith and its application to social ethics, the following discourse addresses difficult situations—and subsequent ethical decisions—concerning persons who are suffering at the end of life.[8] The writer is a confessing Christian and retired physician, who has had a life-long interest in theology and ethics. His credits include a master's degree in theological studies (M.T.S.) and previous writings on the subject at hand. Furthermore, the writer has had personal experiences in making difficult choices for dying family members. His current concern arises from the fact that there is no unanimous opinion—Christian or not—concerning the use of "last resort" options to relieve a patient's suffering at the end of life. These options are reviewed in detail in Chapter Six.

Therefore, this discourse seeks to relate and assess the opinions of Christian men and women who have studied, witnessed, and cared for, these patients.[9] These opinions are the respected "voices"

---

8   See *Random House Dictionary of English Language* (New York, 1987) where *Christian ethics* comes under the following definition: "...rules of conduct recognized in respect to a particular class of human actions or a particular group culture..." Using the word *social* as a modifier expands Christian ethics as follows: "...of or pertaining to the life, welfare and relations of human beings in a *community*...(my emphasis)"

9   I shall use the term "patient" interchangeably with the term "person" throughout this essay, realizing that some individuals suffering at the end of life may or may not be under the immediate care or supervision of a physician. Most dying patients or persons remain under the palliative care of hospital staff, in-home nurses, hospice caretakers, and/or family members.

of physicians, philosophers, theologians, and ethicists who have addressed the sometime dire plight of dying patients. Thus, part of our discussion attempts to evaluate the philosophical and/or religious views of these discerning scholars, who have studied what they believe to be the appropriate ethical responses to patients near death. However, we shall see that the solutions to these situations are not so clear cut: in assessing similar cases, Christians—expert or not—may arrive at different decisions. Thus, the responses to these cases of terminal care can become mired in moral ambiguity[10]. Judgments from these different viewpoints, often under secular influence, may be seen as appropriate by some and inappropriate by others. That is to say that the reaction to suffering at the end of life is often based on an individual viewpoint. This results in a wide range of ethical decisions.

Addressing this moral ambiguity in decision-making, Harmon L. Smith states that Christians have made two "moves" which he interprets as "disastrous" to an authentic moral life.[11] One move is "to reduce vital Christian piety to propositions," and the other is "to suppose that decision-making is the *sine qua non* of the moral life."[12] Dr. Smith adds a critical summary comment:

---

10   The use of the word, "ambiguity," implies "doubtfulness or uncertainty of meaning or intention," such as the requirement that the patient assess her level of pain before the institution of "terminal sedation."

11   Dr. Smith is an Episcopal priest and professor emeritus in Christian and medical ethics at Duke Divinity School.

12   *Where Two or Three Are Gathered: Liturgy and the Moral Life* (Cleveland: The Pilgrim Press, 1995), p. 2. Dr. Smith adds, "Of course, the pervasive tendency nowadays is for Christians and the church to speak of these (moral) matters in ways which are calculated to be congenial and comfortable in the presiding secular environment. This is merely another evidence for why the single largest problem with so much of Christian ethics these days is the extent to which 'Christian' fails to control 'ethics.'" (p. 25)

"Until we recover the awareness that our Christian life is derived from a succession of faithful witnesses upon whom we are dependent, and that prayer and holiness are essential marks of our moral life, we will continue to suppose that Christian responses to the human situation—to war, to sexuality, to racism, and to all other 'moral issues' which require our urgent and faithful attention—are equivalent to Aristotle's understanding of politics as 'the art of the possible.'"[13]

Thus, he stresses the Christian religious viewpoint that avoids moral ambiguity in these "human situations" and rejects the ancient cultural bias which pervades our society today that "anything is possible."

Concerning death and dying, I will present a brief historical discussion of what is considered the essential philosophical, scientific, or religious meanings of "life" and "death." Sarah Franklin, who in 1995 was at the University of California, Santa Cruz, begins with the classical definition of "life," or "vitalism," as formulated by Aristotle, "... life is defined by the possession of a soul, or vital force, through which an entity is rendered animate and given shape."[14] Franklin elaborates further, "This view is known as *entelechy*—a *telos*, an ultimate end that is self-defined as the achievement of a final form."[15] [Modern scientists initially rejected this proposition for its "teleologism" (fusion of an endpoint with a cause) and "essentialism" (predeterminism).] For Aristotle, then, the purpose of life is a "predetermined endpoint...a purpose that is contained in itself, independent of any external causal

---

13   Ibid. p. 2.
14   Franklin, S.: "Life" in *Encyclopedia of Bioethics,* Vol. 3, Reich, W.T., Editor-In-Chief (New York: Simon and Schuster Macmillan,1995), p. 1346.
15   Ibid.

agent."[16] Thus, Aristotle presents life as an end in itself, and he stops short of recognizing an afterlife, admitting that with intelligence humankind has a "spark" of the divine.[17]

Thus, there is something present within the *Homo sapiens* that is beyond, or other than, the purely physical or chemical. My presumption is that this "something" or "spark" is the same as the "soul." In the following discussion, we will comment on the ancient idea that, at death, the soul separates from the body. This raises the question: Has this philosophical duality "contaminated" the biblical view that the resurrected body is a psychosomatic unity—the soul and body are inseparable or only temporarily separated? Ponder this, for we will come back to the question.

With the establishment of Darwin's theory of evolution there "...came a radical new understanding of life: as an underlying connectedness of all living things."[18] This view of Darwin brought to the world's attention the modern notion of "life itself." Thus Franklin writes:

"Life, in the sense of life itself, is thus a concept linked closely to the rise of the modern life sciences, founded on

16   Ibid.
17   See Warner, W.: "Aristotelianism" in *The Encyclopedia of Philosophy*, Vol. 1, Edwards, P., Editor-In- Chief (New York: Macmillan Publishing Co., Inc., and The Free Press, 1967), p.150, where he says that Aristotle has no conception of the Christian idea of "radical redemption" but that for humankind "...philosophic activity was, to be sure, the most precious element of a good life and that in which man (sic) most nearly approaches the blessedness of divinity, but hardly a refuge from this world or a means of access to another." For an opinion of a modern philosopher see Ayer, A.J.: *The Meaning of Life* (New York: Charles Scribner's Sons, 1990), p. 180, where he concludes that there is no consensus as to the meaning of life, rejecting the notion "...of the possibility of the continuance of one's existence, in one form or another, after death."
18   Franklin, S., p. 1347.

notions of evolutionary change, the underlying connectedness of all living things, and a biogenetic mechanism of heredity through which life reproduces itself."[19]

For the purposes of our discourse, however, this scientific explanation is not enough. The Christian and other religious persons see "life" as a moral issue and concern themselves with "... the vitalistic notion of life as something inexplicable and deserving of reverence and protection..."[20] This is getting close to the idea of life as something sacred: that life is a gift on loan from a gracious God and is deserving of the utmost respect in living or dying. This reaches a crescendo for the Christian who believes that we are created in the image of God. As a key fits a lock, the human being is intimately connected to God. God is holy and we aspire to be holy. We can not take life in any arbitrary sense—wasting the gift and disregarding the sacredness. The "meaning of life" for the Christian, as an apostolic witness, is reflected in the triune God who became incarnate in the life, death, and resurrection of Jesus Christ.[21] We will see, then, that all Christian reflection on, or decisions for, end-of-life issues should be based on the ethical example of Christ as "Lord of all." In contrast to this strict application of the Gospel, we shall see that there are Christian theologians, who also espouse this "trinitarian ethic," but conclude that it is consistent with the choice of suicide or assisted death as a means to end a life of extreme suffering. We will discuss this in greater detail in Chapter Four.

---

19   Ibid.
20   Ibid., p. 1348.
21   The "Trinity" or "Triune Godhead," unique to the Christian faith, is defined as a "three in one" deity consisting of God the Father, God the Son, and God the Holy Ghost. It is further defined as the Creator, Redeemer and Reconciler.

This moves us into the traditional concept of death as the loss of the "spirit" or "life force" or "soul" from the body, manifested by the loss of spontaneous respirations, heart beat, and pulse.[22] Even now, with the more modern definition of death as the loss of complete "upper brain function," the loss of the vital "spirit" is still seen by many theologians as the religious explanation of death. Opinions vary as to where the spirit or soul goes after death, but most Christian theologians hold that the believer's soul eventually ends up with a "new" body in "eternal communion" with God. This suggests that this communion with God after death is consistent with psychosomatic unity after a "temporary" separation of the soul from the old body. (My interpretation of this "new" body is that it is an "upgrade" of the old original body. For additional thinking on this "temporary" state after death see what N. T. Wright calls "life after life after death."[23])

But, at any rate, regardless of what happens after death, we move forward and ask a preliminary question: Is it ever appropriate for Christians to choose to intervene in the natural dying process by prematurely ending their own or another patient's life? Under "DEATH: Western Religious Thought," L. D. Kliever, writing from Southern Methodist University, responds:

"Though death is inevitable, it is an event to be held at bay by every possible and honorable means that is not excessively burdensome or morally ambiguous. Therefore, most traditional Jews and Christians are categorically opposed to suicide and active euthanasia , or 'mercy killing.' Since martyrdom is not considered suicide, choosing death

---

22   Kliever, L. D.: "DEATH: Western Religious Thought" in *Encyclopedia of Bioethics,* Vol. 1, p. 511.

23   Wright, N.T.: *Simply Christian: Why Christianity Makes Sense* (New York: HarperOne, 2006), pp. 114-115.

over life in service to one's faith or for the sake of others is allowable if it cannot be avoided in an honorable way."[24]

Thus, the traditional Christian stance is that death is to be "held at bay" and the taking of one's own life or that of another, excepting martyrdom, is wrong and can not be a Christian's choice. Note, however, that "holding life at bay" can not be "burdensome" or "morally ambiguous."

So, when we make a choice in the timing of our or another's death, it is often qualified by any number of different determinates—such as state of consciousness, degree of mental confusion, level of pain, or existential angst—and is easily shrouded in moral ambiguity. These determinates may result in a "bad" (messy) state of dying; this state may be reflected in the caregiver's decisions to add or eliminate terminal therapy. In response to dying, then, it is critical how we view death, vis-à-vis life:

"At best death serves as a motive for creative and responsible life. At worst death looms as a menace to a courageous and generous life. Either way, death lends an urgency to life that would be utterly lacking without it. Death enhances rather than cheapens the value of life."[25]

Many of us—Christian or not—see death as the enemy to be "conquered" and, in that sense, we distort, not only death, but life as well. We fail to remember that life is a gift from God and that only God can take it away. Life is sacred and we can not underestimate its value. Addressing this point further, we will see that some physicians, philosophers, and theologians view dying patients, particularly those with altered consciousness, as having a "diminished" value as a

---

24   Ibid., p 511-512.
25   Ibid., p. 512.

person. To some, then, the usual restrictions to the elimination of life support and the use of terminal therapy are eliminated. To others the patient's value as a person, and healthcare's moral responsibility to that person, dictate otherwise.

With that in view, then, this book will address the question as to whether or not the Christian can ever justify the taking of her own or someone else's life, when either is experiencing severe suffering at the end of life. We will present two answers to the question: (1) based on the discipline and strict application of Christian social ethics, nonviolent resistance would preclude these acts as violations of the universal prohibition against killing and (2) based on a command from God that would override the prohibition against killing, suicide or euthanasia becomes the Christian's option to address extremely rare cases of unrelieved suffering. As we go along, we will ferret out the various components of these answers and bring elucidation to the demands of the question.

In this prologue, how have we set the table? The keys to understanding this discourse include the following: (1) we view the critical aspects of suffering at the end of life from the Christian perspective; (2) we assess the observations and opinions of religious and philosophical scholars who have studied terminal patients *in extremis*; (3) we address the concept and problem of moral ambiguity that occurs as a result of the fact that today the "Christian" in Christian ethics no longer controls ethics; (4) we define "life" and "death" and comment on the critical, yet equivocal, notation that "death enhances rather than cheapens the value of life"; (5) we comment on the conundrum of the "separation" of the body and soul at death; (6) we touched on the subject of the "diminished" value of a patient who has lost some of her vital characteristics and how this might affect how she will be treated and (6) we give two answers to the question as to whether or not the Christian can justify taking her own or another's life when both are experiencing extreme suffering at the end of life.

ACKNOWLEDGMENTS

Before we turn to the introduction to this study, I would like to acknowledge those caring persons who have taught and mentored me during my life, but particularly during my studies at Duke Divinity School. As it relates to the moral life and medical ethics, I would mention Dr. Harmon Smith who was my advisor during my years in the Master of Theological Studies program. He was not only a teacher and mentor, but he became a good friend and golfing partner. Dr. Smith proofread this manuscript and I am forever in his debt. During my brief sojourn later in the Master of Theology (Th.M.) program I would give credit to Dr. Amy Hall, who also was an advisor to me. This book on medical decisions at the end of the Christian's life was born out of Th.M. studies.

Other professors who encouraged me include Dr. Stanley Hauerwas and Dr. David Steinmetz. I mention especially Dr. James Efird who taught me the introduction to the Old and New Testament and *koine* Greek. Greg Duncan, in the admissions office, was always such a friendly advocate for the school and its programs and never stopped supporting me. Finally, I have to give love and credit to my wife, Laura, who was a fantastic alternative to the usual spell-check, and to my daughter, Claire, who was my consulting "technocrat."

INTRODUCTION

HOW CHRISTIANS MAY RESPOND
TO SUFFERING AND BREAKDOWN
OF TABLE OF CONTENTS

For many years, my mother suffered from progressive dementia and carried the diagnosis of Alzheimer's disease. She lived well into her 90's and spent the last years of her life in a nursing home. Eventually, she lost all cognitive brain function, failing to recognize members of her immediate family. I was designated healthcare power of attorney, and I stipulated that she was not to be sent to the hospital for treatment of the expected infections or any other complications of her disease. In each subsequent infection, she responded to the first line of antibiotics. A few weeks before her death she suffered a stroke which left her unconscious—she could not take oral nourishment and required an IV for fluid replacement. No one suggested that we insert a stomach tube for the delivery of nourishment.

As far as we could tell, she was comfortable and free of pain. With the support of the nursing home staff, we made the emotive decision to stop all nutrition and fluid therapy. My mother died quietly in five days. No one will ever know what she died of—her debilitating disease complicated by a stroke or the withdrawal of food and water or a combination of both. For the purposes of our current study, I feel compelled to raise the question: what was the manner of her death? Natural causes, involuntary euthanasia, or unknown? Was it a compassionate thing to do? Was it a violation of the sixth commandment? Was it the Christian thing to do? My Christian friends were unanimous in their support of my decision. They said it was the "right thing to do." What would you have done?

Bearing these questions in mind, I shall present relevant arguments for or against the controversial issues of "unassisted suicide" (US) and "assisted death" (AD) that may be considered because of "extreme suffering" at the end of a Christian's life. Firstly, I use the acronym, "US," to refer to those special end-of-life cases, described by the theologian Karl Barth as "exceptional," where the patient is "commanded" by God to take her own life. Similarly, I use "AD" because, in essence, it characterizes those cases where an "enabler" assists in, or causes, the death of a patient. I mean it to be inherent in the definition of "AD" that (1) the "enabler" is not necessarily a physician, as in physician-assisted suicide (PAS) or physician-assisted death (PAD), (2) the "victim" is not necessarily an immediate patient of a healthcare provider and (3) the death is not necessarily a suicide, but may be a "mercy killing." (Please refer to the glossary where I have attempted to lend some clarity to the acronym "jungle.")

With these definitions in mind, we have to be clear in what it means "to suffer." In the dictionary, it is defined in multiple ways: (1) to undergo or feel pain or distress; (2) to sustain injury, disadvantage or loss; (3) to undergo a penalty, as of death, and (4) to endure pain, disability, death, etc., patiently or willingly.[26] Furthermore,

---

26   Random House Dictionary of the English Language (New York: Random House, 1987).

in the context of requests for PAS, Bascom and Tolle define a new concept, "total pain," as "...the impending disintegration of the person, loss of control, and unresolved spiritual or psychological issues..."[27] Coming from a different perspective, E. J. Emanuel and others note that beyond pain, the primary factors in a patient's desire to end her life are depression and hopelessness, frequent by-products or forerunners of suffering.[28]

In these cases of suffering at the end of life, and in the discussion of US or AD, is there a consideration of the violence that is inherent in these acts? Is one case of suicide or AD more violent that another? What is the "degree" of violence to silently and "mercifully" increase the morphine to a lethal level in a dying patient? One very serious question that rarely comes up is whether or not the patient *in extremis* suffers more violence when she is alive than when she commits suicide or is put to sleep? In my reading of the Christian German theologian, Karl Barth, for example, the violence of the act of suicide by a Christian appears to be an implied consideration.[29] (For an extended analysis of Barth and the exceptional case see Chapter 4.)

We have to be clear, though, that Barth makes a distinction between the suicide that is commanded by God and the suicide that a sinner, out of disobedience, commits as self-murder. This, to me, implies a difference, not only in intent, but also in degree of violence. I think one can read Barth that in his idea of the exceptional case

27 Bascom, P.B. and Tolle, S.W.: "Responding to Requests for Physician-Assisted Suicide," *JAMA* 288 (2002): 95.

28 Emanuel, E. J., et al.: "Attitudes and Desires related to Euthanasia and PAS Among Terminally Ill Patients and their Caregivers," *JAMA* 284 (2000): 2460. I will use a long list of adjectives to describe the type or degree of pain: severe, extreme, unremitting, unresponsive, unnecessary, disabling, overwhelming, dehumanizing, existential, physical, spiritual, psychological, violent, and total.

29 Barth, K.: *Church Dogmatics III/4: The Doctrine of Creation*, Bromiley, G.W. and Torrance, T.F., Editors (Edinburgh: T&T Clark,1961) (By convention used in the notes as "CDIII/4.")

the degree of suffering in taking one's life pales in comparison to the suffering while alive and dying a horrific death. The mercy and compassion of the "saving" act of suicide is reflected in the mercy and compassion of a loving God. Thus, when Barth uses the terms "self-destruction" (CD III/4, p. 401), "annihilation of one's own life" (p. 403) and "self-murder" (p. 404), he never directly elaborates on the violence that is evident and inherent in these acts. I think, though, by context and intent, he clearly implies it and distinguishes these acts from the exceptional case of suicide directly commanded by God. With this extended discussion of suffering and violence, we have set the stage for our analysis of the Christian perspectives on decisions at the end of life.

This discourse begins with the construct and belief that the gospel of Jesus Christ is relevant to these social issues today. We propose that the Christian gospel may be applied to the morality of US or AD as a solution to the problem of extreme and/or unnecessary suffering at the end of life. By implication, it is apparent that palliative care has failed to keep the patient comfortable.[30] John Howard Yoder, the Mennonite theologian, has concluded that the gospel of Jesus Christ is both relevant and normative for this and other social issues today and that the basis for that relevancy is nonviolent resistance.[31] By contrast, Karl Barth, a German theologian, and David Clough, an American theologian, address exceptional cases of suffering in which the patient's condition at the end of life is so overwhelming that the rule of morality against killing is suspended. That opens up the

---

30   Here an important caveat is in order: I purposely exclude those who choose "legal" physician-assisted suicide (PAS), currently available in the states of Oregon and Washington and in legal limbo in Montana.

31   Yoder, J.H.: *The Politics of Jesus* (Grand Rapids: William B. Eerdmans Publishing Company, 1994).

request of US (Barth and Clough) or AD (Clough) as commanded by God and thereby justified?[32, 33]

In laying the foundation for the consideration of these extraordinary issues, then, Chapter 1 begins with an analysis of Yoder's proposal that the witness of Jesus Christ represents the standard for social ethics today. He concludes that this standard is based on the principle of nonviolent resistance. Following this analysis, a subsection entitled, *The Gospel, Strictly Applied*, concerns the application of the apostolic witness to the interpretation of the Gospel. This witness would preclude any acts of suicide or euthanasia. This is followed in Chapter 2 by a discussion of the evolution of "comfort care," defining what Paul Ramsey, a Christian theologian and ethicist, calls "(only) caring for the dying."[34] A subsection of Chapter 2 addresses the moral and theological foundation for this care of the sick and dying.

The historical perspective of PAS and euthanasia, both of which come under the purview of AD, is addressed in two parts in chapter 3. This is followed by a three-part approach, sections 4.1, 4.2, and 4.3, in response to the above question and includes 1) a biblical warrant for the suspension of the prohibition against killing, 2) a

---

32   Barth, K., pp. 397-470. See specifically p. 410 where he refers to "a man (sic) in affliction." See also pp. 356-374 where he discusses health and sickness and refers to the possibility that a sickness and its affects may have to be " 'borne' in the sense that they are drawn by God..." It is on p. 425 that he refers to, but follows with a rejection, a medical case where a doctor is tempted to "...put an end to his (patient's) suffering by helping him (sic) to die..." Thus, Barth would not recognize nor use the term "physician-assisted suicide." He rejects PAS and euthanasia as violations of the sixth commandment, "thou shall not 'kill.'"

33   Clough, D.: "A Theological Framework for End-of-Life Decisions in a Medical Context," Department of Religious Studies, Yale University, New Haven (March 1999).

34   Ramsey, P.: *The Patient as Person: Explorations in Medical Ethics* (New Haven: Yale University Press, 1970).

synopsis of Karl Barth's *Ultima Ratio* (the "ultimate reason") or the exceptional case and 3) an analysis of David Clough's paper on the theology of Barth as it applies to medical decisions at the end of life. Since the issue of "healthcare failure" is important to the question raised, Chapter 5 addresses the definition and essential features of palliative and hospice care at the end of life. This is followed by a presentation in Chapter 6 of how medical science has addressed and expanded the "last resort" options that are available to the sick and dying patient. A prelude to the conclusion, Chapter 7, discusses the complex parameters of "hope" and whether or how "hope" abides when death is near. The eighth chapter responds to and answers the question that we have posed and the final chapter is an Epilogue.

CHAPTER ONE

CHRISTIAN SOCIAL ETHICS

1.1. *THE POLITICS OF JESUS*:
NONVIOLENCE AS NORMATIVE

This subsection, a synopsis of John Howard Yoder's *The Politics of Jesus*, requires attention to the biblical underpinnings of Yoder's claim that the witness of Jesus Christ represents the standard for Christian social ethics. Up until 1972, few theologians or biblical scholars dared to suggest that: (1) "Jesus was…a social critic and an agitator…"[35] and (2) "Jesus…(was) not only relevant but also normative for a contemporary Christian social ethic."[36] But in that year, Yoder published his seminal work and made these two observations. He further explains: "I shall, in other words, be testing the hypothesis that runs counter to the prevalent assumptions: the hypothesis that the ministry and the claims of Jesus are best understood as presenting to men (sic) not the avoidance of political options, but one particular social-political-ethical option."[37]

---

35   Yoder, J.H., p.1.
36   Ibid., p. 11.
37   Ibid.

In an analysis of the life and work of Jesus Christ in the gospel of Luke, Yoder asks one simple question, "Is there a social ethic in this gospel that would be relevant and normative for us today?" In other words, does the Gospel[38] compel the church to be different socially, politically, and ethically? Yoder concedes that "If…Jesus, whoever he was, is no model for ethics, it then becomes immaterial in the detail who he was and what he did."[39]

To support his belief that Jesus is a model for moral inquiry, Yoder presents the following analysis of Luke's gospel: (1) After Mary's cousin, Elizabeth, delights in her expected birth of Jesus, Mary sings a canticle, the "Magnificate." It includes the incredible claim that, "he (the Almighty) has put down the mighty from their thrones and exalted those of low degree (1.52)."[40] Based on these aorist verb tenses[41], this "eschatological reversal"[42] is presented as an accomplished fact, having occurred in the past, but continuing into the future. Yoder comments on the latter sense of the canticle: "In the present testimony of the gospel we are being told that the one whose birth is now being announced is to be an agent of radical social change," and concludes, "…he comes to break the bondage of his people."[43] Fred Craddock, a Lukan scholar, expands on Yoder's notion of radical social change:

"More is involved than the social message and ministry of Jesus in behalf of the oppressed and poor. That will

---

38   When I refer to a specific gospel such as Luke I will use a small "g", but if I am referring to the "message" of Jesus Christ, I will use a capital "G".
39   Yoder. J.H., p. 11.
40   Here Yoder is using the RSV.
41   Craddock, F.B.: *Luke. Interpretation: A Bible Commentary for Teaching and Preaching* (Louisville: John Knox Press, 1990), p.30. Referring to the past tenses (aorist) in the Greek translation, Craddock writes that this "…expresses what is timelessly true: past, present, and future without differentiation."
42   Ibid.
43   Yoder, J.H., pp. 21-22.

follow, to be sure, but here we have a characteristic of the final judgment of God in which there is a complete reversal of fortunes: the powerful and the rich will exchange places with the powerless and poor."[44]

Yoder's analysis of Luke continues: (2) After Jesus has been baptized and tested in the desert, he goes to the synagogue in Nazareth and stands and reads Isaiah 61:1-2:

> "The spirit of the Lord is on me, for he has anointed me to bring the good news to the afflicted. He has sent me to proclaim liberty to captives, sight to the blind, to let the oppressed go free, to proclaim a year of favor from the Lord (Luke 4: 18-19)."

Yoder's interpretation of this passage is one of social revolution, "...the passage from Isaiah 61 which Jesus turns on himself is not only a most explicitly messianic one: it is one which states the messianic expectation in the most expressly social terms."[45] This passage refers specifically to Jesus' reversing the oppression of God's people with the restructuring of their community. He anticipates the coming kingdom, interpreting his role as the Messiah to be one of intervention and renewal for the people of God.[46] Furthermore, this proclaimed, "New Age," is to include the Gentiles as well as the Jews. Thus, it became an all-inclusive movement that filled the scribes and elders "with rage (4:28)."

---

44   Craddock, F.B., p. 30.
45   Yoder, J.H.: pp. 28-29.
46   Ibid. pp. 32-34. For Yoder the year of the Lord, the jubilee, is integral to this "new social reality," the coming kingdom, for "As in the jubilee, and as in the Lord's Prayer, *debt* is seen as the paradigmatic social evil."

Furthermore, (3) Jesus began to teach on the Sabbath (4:31), heal the sick and lame (4:39, 5:24), forgive sins (5:20), and consort with "undesirables" (5:27). He further compounds his problems by selecting from among his associates twelve men to be his disciples (6:12-16). At that point Jesus had become a formal movement and thus a political threat not only to the Jewish establishment, but the Roman as well. "New teachings," Yoder writes, "are no threat, as long as the teacher stands alone; a movement, extending his personality in both time and space, presenting an alternative to the structures that were there before, challenges the system as no mere words ever could."[47]

A critical turn of events occurs in Chapter Nine, when, (4) after the feeding of the five thousand and the confession of Peter that you are "The Christ of God (9:20)," Jesus announces that "The Son of Man must suffer...be rejected...be killed, and on the third day be raised (v.22)." From then on Jesus, "...set his face to go to Jerusalem (v.51)." The crowds began to reject him, because he had become so "hardened" and determined to meet his fate there (v.53).

Thus it is clear to Yoder that Jesus exhibited such human traits as "pride" and was tempted at nearly every turn. But here is the crux of the matter for Yoder and that which separates him from many of his contemporaries:

> "The one temptation the man Jesus faced - and faced again and again - as a constitutive element of his public ministry, was the temptation to exercise social responsibility, in the interest of justified revolution, through the use of available violent methods. Social withdrawal was no temptation to him: that option (which most Christians take part of the time) was excluded at the outset. Any alliance with the Sadducean establishment in the exercise of *conservative*

---

47   Ibid. p. 33.

social responsibility (which most Christians choose the rest of the time) was likewise excluded at the outset."[48]

In the critical chapter, "Trail Balance," (5) Yoder asks the question whether in the story so far has this man Jesus, who did not yield to the temptation of violence, been proven to be authoritative for the church today. If, then, it has been demonstrated that the historical Jesus remains relevant today and the church follows him as the Christ of Faith, what does that have to say to the church about how it relates to the world? To capsule the answer, "The church accepted as a gift the fact that she was a 'new humanity' created by the cross and not by the sword."[49] Thus, this represents an ethic of social responsibility that is epitomized by the authority of the state (Rom.12-13), and the Sermon on the Mount (Mt.5-7). Yoder's analysis of these passages, particularly Romans, challenges Christians"...to be nonresistant in all their relationships, including the social."[50] He continues:

"They *both* (scriptures) call on the disciples of Jesus to renounce participation in the interplay of egoisms which the world calls 'vengeance' or 'justice.' They *both* call Christians to respect and be subject to the historical process in which the sword continues to be wielded and to bring about a kind of order under fire, but not to perceive in the wielding of the sword their own reconciling ministry."[51]

Richard B. Hays, a Christian theologian, a New Testament scholar and current Dean of the Duke Divinity School, puts this idea of Yoder's more succinctly, "To bear the cross as Jesus' follower

---

48   Ibid., pp. 96-97.
49   Ibid., p. 149
50   Ibid., p. 210.
51   Ibid.

is to join the community of those who share his refusal of violence as an instrument of the will of God."[52] Demonstrating further support for Yoder's position, Hays concludes from an analysis of Matthew (5:38-48) that "...the church's embodiment of nonviolence is—according to the Sermon on the Mount—its indispensable witness to the Gospel." Furthermore, from a review of the Pauline literature the same author writes, "There is not a syllable in the Pauline letters that can be cited in support of Christians employing violence."[53] Hays summarizes his research on this subject of nonviolence in the New Testament, "Thus, from Matthew to Revelation we find a consistent witness against violence and a calling to the community to follow the example of Jesus in *accepting* suffering rather than *inflicting* it."[54]

Another witness to the essential nature of nonviolence to the Gospel is Stanley Hauerwas, a Christian theologian and ethicist, who notes: "...the centrality of nonviolence as the hallmark of the Christian moral life" and that "...indeed, nonviolence is not just one implication among others that can be drawn from our Christian beliefs; it is at the very heart of our understanding of God."[55]

John Howard Yoder concludes his book with a capsule of what constitutes Christian social ethics:

"A social style characterized by the creation of a new community and the rejection of violence of any kind is the theme of New Testament proclamation from beginning to

---

52   Hays, R. B.: *The Moral Vision of the New Testament* (HarperSanfransico, 1996), p. 243.

53   Ibid., p. 329 and p. 331.

54   Ibid., p. 332.

55   Hauerwas, S.: *The Peaceable Kingdom* (Notre Dame: University of Notre Dame Press, 1983), pp. xvi and xvii. See p. xxiv where Hauerwas writes: "But the more I read of Yoder the more I was convinced that the main lines of his account of Jesus and the correlative ethic of nonviolence were correct."

end, from right to left. The cross of Christ is the model of Christian social efficacy, the power of God for those who believe."[56]

In summary, the Christian operates under specific rules of ethical or moral conduct exemplified by the life, death and resurrection of Jesus Christ. The cross of Christ, as understood by Yoder's work, requires a resounding "no" to social issues such as US and AD that violate the sixth commandment.[57] Thus Christian ethics reflects a way of communal life that is authoritative for the one who confesses that Jesus Christ is Lord. Thus, for such a person, there is no more serious issue to face than the act of US or AD performed because of suffering at the end of life. In most circumstances the usual moral proscription against such violence holds sway and suicide or euthanasia does not come up in discussions concerning the fate of the dying patient. For the Christian this proscription, as Yoder shows, results from the authority of scripture, the biblical law, and the life and teachings of Jesus Christ.

Yoder's work cannot be brushed aside as the narrow opinion of a Mennonite sectarian theologian. His body of work bears witness to a consistent pattern of thought that stresses the apostolic witness of this man Jesus—inaugurating a new humanity, a new community and a new world. Yoder himself, respecting the tradition of the church and the importance of reason and experience, nevertheless resolves that the scriptures, rightly interpreted, are authoritative. He describes his approach thusly, "The convictions argued here do not admit to being

---

56   Yoder, J.H., p. 242.
57   Add abortion, murder, war, capital punishment, and self-defense as social issues that involve violence.

categorized as a sectarian oddity or prophetic exception. Their appeal is to classical catholic Christian convictions properly understood."[58]

These beliefs, then, call the confessing Christian to confirm and practice nonviolence; therefore, those who recognize and follow the primary apostolic witness of Jesus Christ would not consider, let alone practice, suicide or any form of assisted death.

1.2. THE GOSPEL, STRICTLY APPLIED

One can think of many Christians, some of them martyrs, who followed in the steps of Jesus, exhibiting his social ethic and his practice of nonviolence.[59] One such martyr is the apostle Paul, who wrote to the Roman church, "If we live, we live to the Lord, and if we die, we die to the Lord; so then, whether we live or whether we die, we are the Lord's (Rom. 14:8)." Thus, Paul makes no spiritual distinction between life and death; for, if we are Christ's, our life is holy and at our dying we joyfully await the resurrection of our spiritual bodies (2Cor. 4:14).   Furthermore, Paul, reminds the Corinthians:

"Though our outer nature is wasting away, our inner nature is being renewed every day. For this slight momentary affliction is preparing for us an eternal weight of glory beyond all comparison, because we look not to the things that are seen but to the things that are unseen; for the things

---

58   Yoder, J.H.: *The Priestly Kingdom: Social Ethics as Gospel* (Notre Dame: The University of Notre Dame Press, 1984), p. 9. Here, in the introduction to this book, Yoder is referring to the issues he addressed in *The Politics of Jesus.*

59   Pelican, J.: *Jesus Through the Centuries* (New Haven: Yale University Press, 1985), p. 133. I would be greatly remiss if I did not mention Saint Frances of Assisi as a model for following Jesus.

that are seen are transient, but the things that are unseen are eternal (4:16b-18)."

In other words, we are destined to die a physical death, our mortal flesh will rot away, but the believer's inner being, constantly being made anew, belongs to the heavenly Father through Christ Jesus.

Another such witness for the strict application of the Gospel to life and death was Thomas A' Kempis, an "inmate" in the convent of Mount St. Agnus near Cologne, West Germany, who wrote the *The Imitation of Christ*. Following the words of Jesus recorded in the gospel of John , "I am the light of the world; anyone who follows me will not be walking in the dark but will have the light of Life (8:12)," Thomas said: "let therefore our chiefest endeavor be to meditate upon the life of Jesus Christ."[60] From this perspective Thomas moved to a reflection on life and death, "Labor now to live so, that at the hour of death thou mayest rather rejoice than fear."[61] Following Jesus and walking in the light, we, by his example, live and die in joy.

A. K. Grieb, discussing the identity of Jesus in the book of Hebrews, concludes that "The use of *imitatio Christi* as a warrant for social ethics is pervasive within the New Testament."[62] So, if confessing and imitating Christians have the "light of life," death casts no shadow over their lives.

---

60   Kempis, T.A.: *Imitation of Christ* (New York: Hurst and Company, Publishers, date undetermined), p. 19. I should note the following: (1) Kempis quotes John 8:12 as "He that followeth Me, walketh not in darkness" and (2) the translation of this book "...is chiefly copied from one printed at London in 1677..." p. 9.

61   Ibid., p.66.

62   "'Time Would Fail Me to Tell...': The Identity of Jesus Christ in Hebrews" in Gaventa, B.R. and Hays, R.B., Editors: *Seeking the Identity of Jesus: A Pilgrimage* (Grand Rapids: William B. Eerdmans Publishing Co., 2008), p. 213.

A third example of a Christian martyr—who witnessed to the strict application of the Gospel message—is reflected in the life, imprisonment, and death of Dietrich Bonhoeffer. This German pastor and theologian chafed under the reign of Adolph Hitler.[63] Bonhoeffer left Germany at one point, but, because of an intense sense of loyalty and compassion towards the Confessing Church and the people of Germany, returned to his homeland and joined the conspiracy to kill Hitler. He was executed as a spy and traitor about the time the war was drawing to a close. It has to be said that Bonhoeffer remains a controversial figure, because his part in the conspiracy to kill Hitler contradicted his stance of nonviolence.

Based strictly on the example of Dietrich Bonhoeffer, the reflections of Thomas A` Kempis and the writings of the apostle Paul, the Christian cannot abandon the hope for eternal life and intervene in the natural dying process. Furthermore, we will see that there are rules of care, aligned with these observations, that may reverse an unwarranted fear of death and/or quell any consideration of suicide or AD. To put it another way: many have observed that there is a direct correlation between Gospel-based care at the end of life and overcoming the fear of dying.[64]

---

63   Metaxas, E.: *Bonhoeffer Pastor, Martyr, Prophet, Spy* (Nashville: Thomas Nelson, 2010).

64   Liegner, L.M.: "St. Christopher's Hospice, 1974, Care of the Dying Patient," *JAMA* 234 (1975): 1047-48. During the site visit the author observes: "The lack of suffering, in fact the absolute absence of patient distress, is the unique factor permitting the staff and other patients to overcome their fear of death."

CHAPTER TWO

ETHICS FOR CARE AT THE END OF LIFE

2.1. (ONLY) CARE FOR THE DYING

B riefly, we turn aside to make a distinction between terminal care for the patient at the end of life and care for the patient whose condition is irreversibly extremely poor, but not by the generally accepted term, "terminal." In the world of medicine, then, patients lose one or more of the usual signs of vitality, such as consciousness. (The issue of purposely induced terminal sedation to unconsciousness is dealt with in Chapter Six.) Doctors, philosophers, and even theologians may state that these patients' lives are "diminished." What does this mean? Based on the dictionary definition of "diminished," these writers have concluded that these patients' illnesses have somehow "reduced their lives," have made them seem "less than they were," or have made them seem "less important."[65] If life is considered an absolute value, how can it ever be "less" than it was. Thus, the use of the word, *diminishment,* is unfortunate, misleading and controversial. As it relates to terminal or comfort

---

65   The Random House Dictionary of the English Language (New York, 1987).

care, it is also incomplete, because it does not indicate whether or not the changes in vitality are temporary or permanent. Temporary loss of consciousness is reversible and potentially responsive to therapy. Permanent loss of consciousness, as in persistent vegetative state, is irreversible and unresponsive to therapy that would improve the current state. That argument, making a distinction between permanent and temporary consciousness, carries great weight with doctors and other caregivers. It, however, may not carry any weight with these patients' families who may reject the concept of diminishment altogether. These "vitalists" see only the distinction between life and death and nothing in between. They see breathing and heart function as evidence of life, a life which can not be taken away—only God can do that.

Those persons, including doctors, who stress the importance of the "quality of life," argue that a permanently unconscious patient is better off dead. In this case, the removal of life support is the moral thing to do. There are other signs of loss of "vitality": absent reflexes, markedly impaired vital signs, lack of body movement, or profound dementia. Can, or should, these changes—this decreased state—be quantified? As a summary question we have to ask: "Can this so-called "diminishment" be the basis for the lack of care, the abatement of treatment, the refusal to give life support, or the consideration of suicide or assisted death?"

E. Haavi Morreim wants to "…argue that this dispute about whether physicians ethically can, or ought, *unilaterally*, refuse to provide life support revolves around fundamentally irresolvable moral conflicts concerning our most deeply held beliefs about the value of life, especially profoundly diminished life (my emphasis)."[66] Note that Morreim uses the adverb, "profoundly," to indicate an

---

66   "Profoundly Diminished Life: The Casualties of Coercion," *HCR* 24 (1994): 33.

irreversible state, one that is unresponsive to medical care that would improve the patient's condition. This statement reflects the quandary of today's Christian who may, or should, question the "fundamentally irresolvable moral conflicts" concerning the value of life in a hopelessly dying patient. If our lives are sacred, then the question of who determines whether or not a patient is as valuable as they used to be is futile and invalid.[67] In the end-of-life cases which we are concerned with, the key distinction is that these cases are terminal and the patient may have no more than a few days, weeks, or months to live. On the other hand, patients with permanent unconsciousness may survive for years.

Thus, a religious person has to ask herself: what is the moral foundation for the care of the sick and dying patient? Is that moral foundation pertinent to the patient who does not respond to standard therapy? If this therapy is not pertinent in this type of case, is the cessation of therapy the moral thing to do? The Christian ethicist, accordingly, has to ask: is this moral foundation for the terminally ill patient based on, or consistent with, the life and teachings of Jesus Christ? We now turn to the writing of a Christian and medical ethicist who addressed these questions.

As early as the 1930's, there were those who spoke out against the insensitive "tyranny" of medicine, becoming the "...prophets of an imminent revolution" (that) "...began in 1970 when a Protestant ethicist, Paul Ramsey, published *The Patient as Person*."[68] The thrust

---

67   De la Chaumiere, R.: *What's it All About? A Guide to Life's Basic Questions and Answers* (Sonoma: Wisdom House Press, 2004), p. 34. He writes: "...the very asking of basic questions (of life) has a value," and "that is, it can protect us from an unbecoming forgetfulness of the miracle of being, preserve in us the primordial awe and wonder that anything exists and the sense that *our lives and all of life are sacred* (my emphasis)."

68   Weir, R.F., Editor: *Physician-Assisted Suicide* (Bloomington: Indiana University Press, 1997), p. 47.

of Ramsey's argument is that the patient, no different from the physician, has to be treated with respect as a person. One who "...is an embodied soul or ensouled body..." and "...therefore a sacredness in illness and in...dying."[69] From a religious or spiritual perspective, the physician has to come to understand how she and the patient are related: from birth to death they are part of "...a covenant people on a common pilgrimage."[70] This covenant depends on the fidelity of God to the chosen people and they to God; it is the basis for life, reflecting its sacredness. Ramsey uses the term, "indefectible charity," as "...the ultimate ground for saying that a religious outlook that goes with grace among the dying can never be compatible with euthanasiac acts or sentiments."[71] This charity, effectively and consistently applied as palliative or "comfort" care, emphasizes a deep respect for the process of dying and in many cases can overcome the fear of death or thoughts of ending one's life. In the same vein a physician, in evaluating a patient's request for AD and addressing her concerns and needs, can assure her that she will die peacefully. Thus, kind, caring, and patient empathy in most instances alleviates a patient's desire to end her life.[72]

For Ramsey, then, the moral foundation for the care of the sick and dying derives from traditional medical ethics, which in turn derives from the covenant between the patient and physician. He argues that traditional medical ethics is able to make the necessary discriminating decisions that treat the patient as a person and when cure is no longer possible, result in "...a medical duty to (only) care for the dying."[73] This approach allows for the distinction between the

---

69   Ramsey, P., p. xiii.
70   Ibid.
71   Ibid., p. 153.
72   Curry, L., et al.: "Could Adequate Palliative Care Obviate Assisted Suicide?" *Death Studies* 26(2002): 759.
73   Ramsey, P., p. 116.

"medical imperative" and the "moral imperative" when dealing with the dying patient.[74] These two imperatives, as Ramsey repeatedly notes, are not always synonymous and often directly influence the decision to continue or not the life support of the dying patient. He capsules the distinction:

> "This would require that the doctor lean against his (sic) understanding of the medical imperative in order to keep it optional for his patients; and that as a man who happens also to be a doctor, he should make room for the primacy of human moral judgment on the part of the men who are his patients, the relatives of his patients, and their spiritual counselors to elect life-sustaining remedies or to elect them not."[75]

Thus, Ramsey believes that the highest form of rational inquiry is required of those who would discontinue therapy and institute (only) care for the dying. He states in near summary fashion:

> "Upon ceasing to try to rescue the perishing, one is then free to care for the dying. Acts of caring for the dying are deeds done bodily for them which serve solely to manifest that they are not lost from human attention, that they are not alone, that mankind (sic) generally and their loved ones take note of their dying and mean to company with them in accepting this unique instance of the acceptable death of all flesh."[76]

Bearing this in mind, we have to ask if there are ever any cases or situations where the institution of (only) care for the dying may be modified, qualified or even abandoned? Ramsey says there are two:

---

74   Ibid., p. 124.
75   Ibid.
76   Ibid., p. 153.

(1) "...when they (the dying) are irretrievably inaccessible to human care and (2) "...there is a kind of prolonged dying in which it is medically impossible to keep severe pain at bay."[77] In the second case he adds, "One can hardly hold men (sic) to be morally blameworthy if in these instances dying is directly accomplished or hastened."[78] But, almost immediately, Ramsey counters: "It is of prime ethical importance that we be concerned about the care and protection of all men (sic) in societal and medical practices, and not solely with mercy in individual acts."[79]

In summary, the moral foundation for the care of the sick and dying patient derives from a covenant between the physician and the patient. The covenant is based on an inviolable trust that engenders reciprocal respect between two persons. This foundation and its manifestation, traditional medical ethics, are rooted, then, in the biblical and theological concept of fidelity. As a matter of fact, Ramsey says at the beginning of his book, "...I shall not be embarrassed to use an interpretative principle the (biblical) norm of fidelity to covenant, with the meaning it gives to righteousness between man (sic) and man."[80] In the vast majority of circumstances a "rush to death" is inconsistent with this fidelity covenant. Suggesting the possibility of US or AD, for example, in an individual case of morbid suffering has to give all involved persons, especially Christians, pause to consider the consequences and possible alternatives. We hope that we have shown that the evolution of "traditional medical ethics" provides the basis for care at the end of life. Based on this consideration any desire for suicide or AD is almost always negated.

---

77   Ibid., p. 161 and p. 162.
78   Ibid., p. 163.
79   Ibid., p. 164.
80   Ibid., p. xii.

2.2. THEOLOGICAL BASIS FOR (ONLY)
CARE FOR THE DYING

It is important to present the normative[81] force behind Ramsey's (only) care for the dying. As I have stated, the major thrust of my argument—in consideration of suicide or AD at the end of life—is that the Gospel remains both relevant and normative for Christian social ethics today. Thus, the Gospel would have pertinence to, and authority for, decisions that Christians would have to make with a dying patient. In this context, "social ethics" refers to how the Christian community practices its faith, how it treats its members, and how it treats sick and dying patients. Ramsey has argued persuasively that this normative force lies behind all care at the end of life.

In that vein, further testimony comes from Richard B. Hays, who writes that the "…identity (of this community) is constituted by its confession that the New Testament is normative."[82] The Church, in confessing that its faith and practice is based on the life and teachings of Jesus Christ, bears witness to the timeless truth of the New Testament scriptures. For the Christian this truth is an alternate reality that determines what living in this world means now and what the next world would be like. "Thus, normative Christian ethics is fundamentally a hermeneutical enterprise: it must begin and end in the interpretation and application of Scripture for the life of the community of faith."[83]

---

81   Normative…"of or pertaining to a norm, especially an assumed norm regarded as the standard of correctness in behavior, speech, writing, etc."

82   Hays, R.B., p. 10.

83   Ibid.

This scriptural "truth," as it is "filtered" through the hermeneutical lens of the New Testament scholar lies, as we have said, behind the way we live our lives. This allows for the richness and diversity of our faith. So that means that Christians claim an "authority" for the scriptures. This specific authority is based on the belief that the Bible is the "live word of the living God."[84] Christians further believe that the Bible is revelatory, that it is the self-disclosure of God, who creates, sustains, redeems, and reconciles the world.[85] It calls us to a different way of living and dying, a way that is indicative of the eschatological hope that we will be resurrected when Christ comes again. Thus the Bible is the normative force behind what Ramsey calls "indefectible charity," reflecting the compelling belief that our covenant with God is manifested by our righteousness to each other. This righteousness would never allow us to consider "euthanasiac acts or sentiments."[86] We now turn to a consideration of AD through an historical lens, helping us to understand how we got where we are today.

---

84   Brueggemann, W.: "Biblical Authority," *The Christian Century* (January 3-10, 2001): 14.
85   Ibid., p. 15.
86   Ramsey, P., pp. xii and 153.

CHAPTER THREE

HISTORICAL PERSPECTIVES
ON ASSISTED DEATH

3.1. JANET ADKINS: DYING BEFORE HER TIME

It has been more than two decades since Janet Adkins, a 54 year-old Oregon woman, committed suicide with the assistance of Dr. Jack Kevorkian, a retired Michigan pathologist known as "Dr. Death." She "suffered" from the early stages of Alzheimer's disease;[87] she wanted "...to save herself and her family from the debilitating effects of the disease."[88] She played tennis a few days before she was attached to Dr. Kevorkian's machine, designed to deliver a paralyzing dose of curare and a lethal dose of potassium chloride. It was and is very effective and "advertised" as compassionate!

---

87   See Keck, D.: *Forgetting Whose We Are: Alzheimer's Disease and the Love of God* (Nashville: Abingdon Press,1996), p.15, where he says, "Alzheimer's is a particular type of lethal disease, and because it confronts us with a sustained dying, it is an inescapable reminder that we will all die."

88   Duntley, M.A.: "Covenantal Ethics and Care for the Dying," *The Christian Century* (December 4, 1991): 1136.

In the spring of 1993, the writers of *Newsweek* magazine interviewed Dr. Kevorkian and asked him, "What's the mood when patients are in the process of ending their suffering?" He responded: "It's a strange phenomenon. Not one of them fears death, not one. I've had all kinds of religions, and not one wanted a religious consultation. *Religion is totally irrelevant to what they want* (my emphasis)."

This last comment contradicts important points concerning death and religion that have been cited in the contemporary literature: (1) that there is an exaggerated fear of dying in the Western mind,[89] (2) that a significant number of patients ask for "the presence of clergy" at the end of life[90] and (3) that religion remains relevant to what people want when they are suffering from a terminal illness.[91]

If what Dr. Kevorkian says is true, then, he had a select group of people who were out of the religious mainstream. He made these cases sound as if the patient made a free and rational decision, but we have no evidence that there had been any psychiatric evaluation

---

89   See Callahan, D.: "Pursuing a Peaceful Death," *HCR* 23 (July-August 1993): 35-36, and Shuman. J.: "Constancy: Being Sick and Dying as We Have Lived," in *The Body of Compassion* (Boulder: Westview Press, 1999) p.134-142.

90   Steinhauser, K. E.: "Factors Considered Important at the End of Life by Parents, Family, Physicians and Other Care Providers," *JAMA* 284 (2000): 2479-81. In this article see Table 4 and accompanying text: a broad variation in response to the attribute, "meet with clergy member." However, the number of respondents who agreed with the attribute was as follows: patients (69%), family members (83%), physicians (60%), and other care providers (70%).

91   Ibid. See table 5 and the text where "coming to peace with God" ranked second in nine preselected attributes.

assessing the degree of depression, guilt, anxiety, or other manifestation of mental stress or illness.[92] Is Kevorkian a strange blip on the timeline of history, or is the "need" he filled a result of broad-based societal failure to inform and care for those with chronic life-threatening diseases? Incredibly, Janet Atkins was not truly "suffering" from what was diagnosed as Alzheimer's disease and had not lost her "persona" at the time of her death. How was this diagnosis of a lethal disease made? How much of what she did was related to misinformation, exaggerated reaction or underlying depression, we will never know. These actions of Jack Kevorkian have proven to be a stimulus that has led to the Michigan state law banning PAS as murder. They have created an impetus to national reform in the care of the patient with a chronic disease that is, or becomes, terminal.[93] Since then the states of Oregon and Washington have passed "Death with Dignity" citizen initiatives that allow physicians to assist terminal patients, who fulfill certain criteria, to commit suicide. These two initiatives are not transparent, but the principals in Oregon, for instance, claim that there has been no abuse of the laws. In addition, and sometimes in parallel with PAS—Oregon is a good example—"Palliative care and hospice have improved in terms of access and delivery, and they remain the standards of care for addressing the suffering of seriously ill and terminal patients."[94]

---

92   My reading of press reports.

93   See Scherer, J.M. and Simon, R.J.: *Euthanasia and the Right to Die: A Comparative View,* (Lanham, Md.: Rowman and Littlefield Publishers, 1999), p.11. These authors note that Kevorkian assisted in nearly 100 suicides, had his medical license suspended, was prosecuted twice for murder, went to prison, went on a hunger strike, and was released so that he would not die a martyr. The fact that both murder cases were dismissed led to Michigan passing a law banning PAS as murder.

94   Quill, T.E.: "Physician-Assisted Death in the United States: Are the Existing 'Last Resorts' Enough?" *HCR* 38 (2008): 17.

3.2. FROM ANCIENT GREECE TO JOSEPH FLETCHER

In the preface to a book on PAS the editor, Robert F. Weir, Ph.D., states, "…it is one of the perennial ethical problems in medicine."[95] The public's interest in PAS, as an ethical problem, has waxed and waned, dependent on certain historical events, social forces, and outspoken individuals or groups. But PAS and, to a lesser degree, euthanasia have never been too far from the public's collective consciousness.

Today, "…the debates surrounding euthanasia and PAS have focused on the wish for control and influence over the manner and timing of one's death."[96] Historically, this phenomenon of controlling one's destiny and death goes back a long way, for, "…in ancient Greece…persons regarded suicide as a means of escaping painful illness and suffering that accompanied dying."[97] These suicides were accomplished by taking a lethal amount of a drug often obtained "…from someone identifying himself (sic) as a physician."[98]

Compare this ancient scenario to the situation at the beginning of the nineteenth century when, "…Americans of all walks of life could procure laudanum or any number of unpatented medicines filled with opium or its active alkaloid, morphine, without relying on doctors."[99] Thus, dying could be "controlled" at home without

---

95   Weir, R.F., Editor: *Physician-Assisted Suicide* (Bloomington: Indiana University Press, 1997), p. vii. As Weir notes, PAS is also "…an issue that involves law and public policy."

96   Scherer, J.M. and Simon, R.J., p.vii.

97   Weir, R.F., p. vii. This needs some elaboration: what Weir says is true to a point, for ancient Greece was sympathetic to individuals who considered suicide as a form of relief from suffering at the end of life. However, in that society there remained "qualifications" for, and "taboos" against, suicide. Furthermore, one needed the state's permission to commit suicide. See also Scherer, J.M. and Simon, R.J., pp. 1 and 2.

98   Ibid.

99   Vanderpool, H.Y.: "Doctors and the Dying of Patients in American History" in Weir, R.F., p. 34.

the need or service of a doctor. However, "controlled" dying at home didn't last very long because, organized as the American Medical Association in 1847, physicians responded quickly to gain control of the dying patient. They began to insist "...on quiet, composed, and hope-imbued surroundings...as the most effective means of prolonging life..."[100]

One of the reasons for the latest interest in suicide and AD is the threat of "abusive" modern medical technology and the specter of dying alone.[101] Thus, this shift in the control of death from the family to the doctor is critical to our understanding of the current controversy and the "tyranny" of medicine.[102] By the turn of the twentieth century this shift was aided by the fact that the Federal Government was beginning to control narcotics.

At the same time it became evident that American physicians and others were beginning to draw a distinction between PAS and euthanasia, and even some groups were beginning to soften their stance on the prohibition against assisted suicide. For in the midst of restating the AMA's opposition to euthanasia in 1904, one of its editors commented, "We may excuse the person who commits suicide to avoid inevitable torture or dishonor." Obviously, it is highly significant for a physician at that time to describe dying in this way, admitting to medicine's inability to prevent the pain and suffering that may occur with death. In 1904 physicians had few resources to combat such prevalent diseases as heart attack, stroke, cancer, and systemic infection.

---

100   Weir, R.F., p. 37.
101   Steinhauser, K.E., et.al: "Factors Considered Important at the End of life by Patients, Family, Physicians and Other Care Providers," *JAMA* 284 (November 15, 2000): 2479. See Table 2 where greater than seventy percent of all participants rated the attribute, "Not Die Alone," as important at the end of life.
102   Weir, R.F., p.47.

But, eventually, as the physician gained the wherewithal to combat these diseases, other problems resulted from the newly emerging medical therapies. H.Y. Vanderpool, Ph.D., Th.M., discusses these problems under the heading of the "Dreadfulness of Hospitalized Dying."[103] For by the 1950's, with total control in the hospital, the doctor had diagnostic and therapeutic advances at her disposal that allowed her to treat a patient, sometimes to cure, but oftentimes to prologue life indefinitely.[104] This ability to forestall death in the special care units became known as the "ICU Syndrome" and it struck fear in the hearts of those who wanted to die at home surrounded by family.

What, then, were the physicians to do when it became evident that cure was impossible and they had to let the patient die? They knew that "...dying must be painless and peaceful," and in some cases they found ways to do that.[105] Weir cites a report[106] from 1965 that stated:

"The countenancing of suicide continued. Called 'auto-euthanasia,' suffering patients were at times relegated to a separate 'dying room,' where with or without a 'nurse's surreptitious assistance' (via providing pills at the bedside and leaving the patient 'unwatched for comparatively long periods of time') the patient could and would 'manage his (sic) own death.'"[107]

---

103   Vanderpool, H.Y., in Weir, R.F., p.43.
104   Ibid., pp.45-46. Vanderpool adds, "Physicians, therefore, became life's appointed guardians."
105   Ibid., p 45.
106   See Callahan, D.: "Medical Technology and the Human Future: Slippery Slope," *The Christian Century* (2002): 40. He writes: "The decade (of the 60's) witnessed the advent of kidney dialysis, organ transplantation, the birth-control pill, intensive-care units, the artificial respirator, prenatal diagnosis..."
107   Vanderpool, H.Y., in Weir, R.F., p. 45.

Furthermore, a few patients who wanted to die, but could not manage their own death, were put to "sleep" by a lethal dose of narcotic.[108] Thus, there were cases where one could not make a distinction between suicide and euthanasia.[109] Dying had become a private matter dependent on circumstances controlled by the patient and/or healthcare provider. The families, certainly the physicians, were relieved of the necessity of their care and presence; therefore, a number (any number is significant) of hospital patients died unattended. Vanderpool concludes, "All, or at least all, of the expectations and meanings of death that had sustained Nineteenth-century Americans' belief that to witness a person's passage from life was a 'great privilege' had been lost."[110]

In 1970 the public became enthralled with Joseph Fletcher and situation ethics. His utilitarian, means-to-an-end philosophy stressed the importance of the "quality of life" over the "value of life."[111] Weir rightly concludes, "No single individual championed the cause of physician-administered death more than Joseph Fletcher…for (whom) quality-of-life concerns morally justify our 'taking it into our own hands to hasten death for ourselves (suicide) or for others (mercy killing)'"[112]

108　Ibid.
109　Being a pathologist and former medical examiner, I find it very interesting that the cause and manner of death in cases like these have to be falsified on the death certificate. It puts the attending physician and/or medical examiner in a compromising position with legal implications.
110　Vanderpool, H.Y., in Weir, R.F., p.45.
111　Ibid., p. 53.
112　Ibid., p. 52. See also Scherer, J.M. and Simon, R.J., p.7, where Fletcher opined that murder required "malice aforethought," while euthanasia required "mercy aforethought." His "quality-of-life" (morality of life) position does not necessarily translate into a "quality-of-death" (morality of death) position.

So, do we conclude that what we are about, i.e., Christian social ethics, is purely academic and of no practical application? In the current climate PAS is either condoned and performed illegally or supported by state stature and performed legally.[113] Why, then, should we bother to argue the moral or religious tenants of the issue at all? There are those who argue for the need to prevent "insensitivity" to the privilege of witnessing the natural death of a patient. Others want to keep open the argument that sanctioning PAS will lead to a further slide into a national consensus on mercy killing. But regardless of the argument one wants to make, in the current climate, there will continue to be surreptitious deaths. Palliative and hospice care is now the standard of care at the end of life and is the first line of defense against the "need" to consider suicide or mercy killing. We cannot opt out of the arguments that consider the moral or religious aspects of end-of-life decisions. This is particularly true when we consider the arguments for justification of suicide and/or AD—those arguments have to stand the test of philosophical and theological debate.

---

113   Scherer, J.M. and Simon, R.J., p.11. The Oregon Death with Dignity Act passed by a margin of 52 to 48%. Now in 2008 the state of Washington passed a similar act. See Berlinger, N.: "Helping People Out," *HCR* 39(January-February 2009): last, but unnumbered page, where she notes "...Montana may be next, via case law."

CHAPTER FOUR

JUSTIFICATION FOR UNASSISTED SUICIDE OR ASSISTED DEATH

4.1. SUSPENSION OF THE ETHICAL NORM

From the Christian perspective, is there ever a biblical and theological warrant to suspend the ethical norm against killing in favor of a command of God to commit self-murder (US) or perform a mercy killing (AD)? This question may be asked in a different manner: do we have an absolute duty to God, which, by commanding a person to kill herself or another, would in very unusual circumstances override the universal ethic against killing?[114]

---

114   See *The New Interpreter's Bible* (Nashville: Abingdon Press, 1994). This ethic derives from the sixth commandment: "Thou shall not murder" with an alternate reading "Thou shall not kill." The Hebrew word used, *rasah,* is interpreted by most scholars as murder. Traditionally, the distinction between murder and killing rests on motive, asking the question: "Was the killing intentional, premeditated, willful, and treacherous (p. 863)?" However, Karl Barth and others interpret the sixth commandment as "reverence for life." "Appeal to Gen. 9:6 suggests that biblical faith has drawn an uncompromising line against the taking of another life, period. Human life is intrinsically of value and may not be ultimately violated (p. 848)."

The classical circumstances in the Bible that relate to this question occur in the story of Abraham and the sacrifice of Isaac, the Aqedah (Gen. 22:1-19).[115] One of the most extensive analyses of this story and its conundrum occurs in Soren Kierkegaard's work, *Fear and Trembling*, written in 1843. This Danish philosopher and theologian addresses the issue of the sacrifice of Isaac primarily by asking two questions: (1) "Is there a teleological suspension of the ethical?" and (2) "Is there an absolute duty **to** God?"[116] To consider these questions I present a brief exegetical analysis of the text from Genesis. There, chapter 22 begins with: "After these things…(v. 1a)" These things that occurred in the previous chapter include the fact that Abraham's son, Isaac, is born; Abraham's first son, Ish'mael, and his mother, Hagar, are banished to the wilderness; and Abraham makes a covenant with Abimelech and sojourns many days in the land of the Philistines.

These events are important in the transition to Chapter 22: (1) Isaac is now Abraham's "only son," (2) Abraham completes and keeps a covenant and (3) Abraham remains an alien in the land in which he will be a "great nation" (18:18). "After these things God tested Abraham…(22:1a)." Only God knows why Abraham has to

---

115   The Hebrew word for "binding." See "Aqedah" in *The Oxford Companion to the Bible,* edited by Metzger, B.M., and Coogan, M.D. (New York and Oxford: Oxford University Press, 1993), p. 43-44.

116   Kierkegaard, S.: *Fear and Trembling/Repetition* (Princeton: Princeton University Press, 1983), pp. 54-67 ("Problema I") and pp. 68-81 ("Problema II"). See Amy Hall's discussion of this work in *Kierkegaard and the Treachery of Love* (Cambridge: Cambridge University Press, 2002), pp. 54-81. She states: "While *Fear and Trembling* is about sin, duplicity, and our need for graced forgiveness, it may return to the reader as a text about ethics, the untranslatable obligation of the individual before God alone, and God's judgment against an idolatry that fuses self and other (p.54)," and "The most fundamental and thus prior relationship for which I exist and for which my beloved exists is the God-relationship (p. 55)."

be "tested," but it may be the only way that God and Israel can move into the future with mutual trust.[117] In some sense "tested" means that God "tempted" Abraham. How was he tempted? The greatest temptation for Abraham would be for him to disobey God and save his son. For Kierkegaard the word "test" may be used in the sense of "ordeal" or "trial."[118]   And God said, "…Abraham (22:1b)!" After Abraham responded that he was there, God said, "Take your son, your only son Isaac, whom you love, and go to the land of Moriah, and offer him there as a burnt sacrifice upon one of the mountains that I shall show you (v.2)."[119] So Abraham did as he was told and took a donkey, wood, a knife, two young men, and Isaac to the foot of Mount Moriah. The key phrase in this sequence is "take… your only son Isaac, whom you love…" God is here recognizing the command that a father love his son and love him unconditionally, as God loves Abraham. (We have seen that Abraham has already "lost" one son, but that event does not mean that Abraham would stop loving Ish'mael.)

With the mountain in sight, Abraham says a puzzling thing to the young men who went along with him, "Stay here with the donkey; the boy and I will go over there; we will worship and then we will come again to you (v. 5)." Are we to take this at face value: Abraham did intend to worship and return with Isaac unharmed? Or did Abraham sense fear in the young men and Isaac? Therefore, Abraham might have felt compelled to break the tension and simply say that he and Isaac were going up on the mountain to worship God and return forthwith.

---

117   Some later Jewish texts reason that Satan may have questioned Abraham's devotion to God.

118   Kierkegaard, S., p. 9. See accompanying note on p. 341. In philosophical terms the ordeal, the spiritual trial, involves, in the case of Abraham, having to choose between the lesser (the ethical) and the greater (the absolute duty).

119   From the NRSV.

But Isaac asks a question, "...where is the lamb for a burnt offering (v.7)?" Again we have a puzzling response from Abraham, "God himself will provide the lamb...(v.8)" As we noted above, we cannot be sure of what Abraham is thinking, but the reasonable guess is that he is reassuring Isaac and/or simply stating his faith that God will provide the lamb. Still, at this point, are we not to presume that Abraham intends to follow God's command to sacrifice Isaac on the altar?[120] It may be that there is another explanation for Abraham's "confidence" that Isaac will be saved. In the exegesis of the book of Hebrews, Grieb states, "Repetition of 'by faithfulness (*pistis*)' links Abraham (*who trusted God's ability to create Isaac and to raise him from the dead*) and Moses...(my emphasis)."[121]

After Abraham prepared the altar and "bound" Isaac for the burnt offering, "...he reached out his hand and took the knife to kill (or, "to slaughter") his son (v.10)," but the angel of the Lord intervened and said to Abraham, "Do not lay your hand on the boy...for now I know that you fear God since you have not withheld your son, your only son, from me (v.12)." Then God (or the angel) does provide a ram and Abraham "...offered it up as a burnt offering instead of his son (v.13)." The remainder of the story (vv.14-19), once God is convinced of Abraham's faith, deals with God's blessing, "I will indeed bless you, and I will make your offspring as numerous as the stars of heaven and as the sand that is on the seashore (v.17)."

Kierkegaard writes about Abraham, "He gets Isaac back again by virtue of the absurd."[122] This absurdity manifests itself in the form of a conflicting and illogical double command: Abraham, the father

---

120 The question has been raised: why is the story of Abraham and the sacrifice of Isaac not more about the prohibition against human sacrifice, particularly child sacrifice? Viewed differently, an additional question has been raised concerning the possibility that the story has been seen as an impetus to violence against children.
121 Grieb, A.K., p. 204.
122 Ibid. p. 57.

of Isaac shall love his son, *his only son,* and Abraham, standing in the fear of God, shall take his son and offer him as a burnt sacrifice to God. Even in the face of the "ethical" temptation to save his son, Abraham would sacrifice Isaac because of the higher "absolute" command. We have noted that it appears that Abraham may have had a "faithful" expectation that a ram would be provided and he would not have to decide between saving Isaac and following the command of God.

In commenting on Luke 14:26, i.e., "Whoever comes to me and does not hate his father and mother," Kierkegaard capsules what Abraham is about, "The absolute duty can lead one to do what ethics would forbid, but it can never lead the Knight of faith (Abraham) to stop loving."[123] Finally, Kierkegaard explains the relationship between temptation and duty:

> "It (what Abraham faces on Mount Moriah) is an ordeal, a temptation. A temptation - but what does that mean? As a rule, what tempts a person is something that will hold him (sic) back from doing his duty, but here the temptation is the ethical itself, which would hold him back from doing God's will. But what is duty? Duty is simply the expression for God's will."[124]

Based on Kierkegaard's analysis of the story of Abraham and Isaac we have presented a situation demonstrative of a biblical warrant to suspend the ethical prohibition against murder in the face of an absolute duty to obey God's will.

Thus, today, we may be commanded to address exceptional cases of extreme suffering where the relative good (the ethical) is trumped

---

123   Ibid., p. 74.
124   Ibid., p. 60.

by the absolute good (the command of God).[125] Other philosophers and theologians have commented on the issue of how to view the exceptional or catastrophic case: (1) Charles Fried writes, "I believe, on the contrary, that the concept of the catastrophic is a distinct concept just because it identifies the extreme situation in which the usual categories of judgment (including the category of right and wrong) no longer apply,"[126] and (2) Richard A. McCormick writes, "We know, for instance, that killing of others is, except in the most extreme and tragic circumstances, destructive of the humanum in every way, and is therefore destructive of community."[127]

As in the comments by Fried and McCormick, Karl Barth has written of the "catastrophic," the "extreme," and the "tragic" in his analysis of the Ultima Ratio, the "last argument" for the exceptional case.

4.2. *ULTIMA RATIO*: THE EXCEPTIONAL CASE FOR UNASSISTED SUICIDE

Before we begin our analysis of Karl Barth and the *Ultima Ratio*, a further elaboration on the term, "assisted death (AD)," is in order. To

---

125   Ibid., p. 68. See also note 1 on page 349 concerning God as the highest good: "Kant's denial of an absolute duty to God transcending rational morality (or a conflation of divine will and the autonomy of man's (sic) rational will) is shared with variations by Fichte, Schleiermacher, and Hegel. In raising the question, Johannes de Silentio (Kierkegaard) runs counter to the dominant ethical thought of the time."

126   Fried, C.: *Right and Wrong* (Cambridge, Mass.: Harvard University Press, 1978) p.10.

127   McCormick, R.A.: "Ambiguity in Moral Choice" from The Pere Marquette Theology Lecture (1973): 24. For some idea of the very limited number of cases of extreme suffering that may override the usual prohibition against killing, see Bascom, P.B. and Tolle, S.W., p. 91, where "only 1% of dying patients specifically request it (PAS)" and of those, only "1 in 10" commit suicide.

make a specific clarification, in contrast to Barth's idea of unassisted suicide (US) as a "command from God," the category of AD would include those cases where a physician, other healthcare worker, family member, or friend would, at the request of the patient, assist in or cause the death of the patient who is in extreme suffering at the end of life. This independent action may or may not be outside the state law and, thus, has to be distinguished from the legal practice of PAS in the states of Oregon and Washington and from the legal practice of "voluntary" euthanasia in the Netherlands.[128] In this setting, the practice of PAS or euthanasia has to adhere to a specific set of requirements instituted by the laws of these states and this country. With this brief elaboration of the distinction between US and AD, it is my intent to make it clear that Barth would not countenance AD, considering, but rejecting, these killing acts as violations of the sixth commandment.

In the context of our discourse, therefore, we are analyzing Barth's idea of the "last argument" as he has applied it to certain cases of unassisted suicide by a seriously ill patient, presumably beyond effective medical care. Here we have to understand what Barth considers the role of the doctor in the arena of health and sickness: firstly, the relationship between the patient and the doctor is limited by the fact that God-given health "…is the strength to be as a (sic) man;"[129] secondly, Barth is emphatic that in this sense of the "health" of a person, the doctor is limited in what she can do; thirdly,

---

128 It should be noted that the legality of voluntary euthanasia is sometimes reversed: in 1997 the Australian Parliament overturned the legalization of euthanasia in the Northern Territory. See Daniel Callahan's opinion in "Organized Obfuscation: Advocacy for Physician-Assisted Suicide," *HCR* 38(September-October, 2008): 30-32, where he points out that the physicians in the Netherlands have found themselves on the "slippery slope" of involuntary or non-voluntary euthanasia. He observes that they obscure the definition of "voluntary euthanasia" and claim they are misunderstood by outside observers.

129 Barth, K., p.357.

he is clear that, rightly, the patient should, when she considers it necessary, seek a consultation with a doctor; fourthly, the doctor "deserves trust rather than suspicion, not an absolute confidence, but a solid relative confidence that in this matter he (sic) has more general information than we have…;"[130] fifthly, it may be the case that, after treatment, the sick individual "is well again at least in the medical sphere;"[131] and lastly—in my reading of "Respect for Life" in CD III/4, this is as close as it gets to terminal care—the doctor, if having done her best for the patient,

"…cannot extend the limits of life available, (she) can at least make the restrictive ailment tolerable, or at worst, if there is no remedy and the limits become progressively narrower, (she) can do everything possible to make them relatively bearable."[132]

Beyond this, the patient may be called or commanded to take her own life. Barth does not consider these rare and unusual cases of suicide violations of the sixth commandment. Elaborating further, he states:

"…the Gospel makes it quite plain that there is no such thing as a free choice of death. Suicide in the sense of self-murder can only be condemned. While there can be no doubt about this, we must not forget the exceptional case. Not every act of self-destruction is as such suicide in this sense. Self-destruction does not have to be the taking of one's own life."[133]

---

130   Ibid., p. 362.
131   Ibid.
132   Ibid.
133   Ibid., p. 410.

For Barth, then, the exceptional case arises from the theological precept that this life, and the life which is to come, represent a command, equivalent to "I shall," from God our creator.[134] It is a mystery, but life is a gracious gift from a loving God. For each human being, life remains a "loan" from our creator and with that "loan" comes the responsibility to value and protect that human life. Thus life, as a good among other goods, does not represent, as Albert Schweitzer proposed, the "supreme good." Barth responds, "Where Schweitzer places life we see the command of God."[135] Barth, then, reiterates that we worship the one God and that we cannot worship "life" as if it were a "second god."[136]

The biblical basis for this view of God and the gift of life is heavily influenced by Barth's interpretation of Paul's letter to the Romans.[137] In 1918, when Barth wrote his commentary on Romans, his readers raised the question of "a system" and he answered, espousing the fundamentals of both his theology and philosophy:

"My reply is that, if I have a system, it is limited to a recognition of what Kierkegaard called the 'infinite qualitative distinction' between time and eternity (between

---

134   Read Nigel Biggar's reflections on Barth's trinitarian ethics in Webster, J., Editor, *The Cambridge Companion to Karl Barth* (Cambridge: The Cambridge University Press, 2000), p. 212.

135   Barth, K., p. 324. Thus life as the "supreme good" would become the "criterion of all virtue."

136   Ibid., p. 342.

137   Barth, K.: *Epistle to the Romans*, Hoskyns, E. C. and Cumberlege, G., translators (London, New York, and Toronto: Oxford University Press, 1950). See also Hauerwas, S.: *With the Grain of the Universe* (Grand Rapids: Brazos Press, 2001), p.152, where Hauerwas writes: "That book (*Epistle to the Romans*) not only changed Barth's life, but changed the world of theology...Barth was doing no more than reminding us that what is wrong with the world is its failure to acknowledge that God is God...The conceptual and moral implications of the claim that God is God and that we are not would occupy the rest of Barth's life and work."

41

humankind and God), and to my regarding this as possessing negative as well as positive significance: 'God is in heaven, thou art on earth.' The relation between such a God and such a man (sic) and the relation between such a man and such a God, is for me the theme of the Bible and the essence of philosophy. Philosophers name this KRISIS of human perception—the Prime Cause: the Bible beholds at the same cross-roads—the figure of Jesus Christ."[138]

Therefore, in this relation between God and humankind (or vice-versa), it is clear that this human being, "on earth," has finite qualities that limit what she may do and be—in that sense she has limited "value"—and thus, she may be called to suicide as an exceptional case.[139]

Explaining further, it is in the realm of what Barth calls the "frontier of life," a decision point, where one has to choose between life and death. It is in the context of this choosing, knowing that each one may be good or bad, that one may consider the exceptional case by virtue of the *ultima ratio*. Here the possibility exists that under certain circumstances God would command a Christian to violate the sixth commandment and commit suicide.[140] Barth explains the "frontier" of life:

"The one God, who is of course the Lord of life and death, the Giver of this life and that which is to come, will in all circumstances and in every conceivable modification

138   Ibid., p. 10.
139   Here the question comes before us again: What is the 'value' of human life? Barth sees the value of human life as it stands in relationship to the supreme God in heaven above. In the end the human bides her time and waits for the command from God which, in essence, may say that the value of her life is seen in the taking of her life.
140   Ibid., pp. 400-413.

demand respect for life. He will never give man (sic) liberty to take another view of life, whether his own or that of others. Indifference, wantonness, arbitrariness or anything else opposed to respect cannot even be considered as a command or even permitted attitude. Even the way to these frontiers—the frontiers where respect for life and the will to live can assume in practice very strange and paradoxical forms, where in relation to one's own life and that of others it can only be a matter of that relativised, weakened, broken and even destroyed will to live—will always be a long one which we must take thoughtfully and conscientiously, continually asking and testing whether that *ultima ratio* really applies. The frontiers must not be arbitrarily advanced in any spirit of frivolity or pedantry; they can be only reached in obedience and then respected as such."[141]

That is to say: when the degradation of our physical being threatens our ability to enjoy and pursue our spiritual being, when the protection of life becomes extremely onerous, when we have tested again and again the command of God and our obedience to it, and when our will to live has been severely compromised, then we may have hit the frontier or decision point of our earthly existence. At this frontier, as the truly exceptional case, the Christian in obedience may perceive that God is commanding that the greatest protection of her life may be unassisted suicide.[142] The essential theological tenant behind this command is

141   Ibid., p. 343.
142   Ibid., p. 398. "But since human life is of relative greatness and limited value its protection may also consist *ultima ratio* in its surrender and sacrifice. In certain circumstances, should the commanding God so will it, it may have to break and discontinue the defense of life in which it should present itself until the boundary is reached."

that only God may give life and only God may take it away. To put it another way: circumstances, particularly a terminal disease, that threaten our ability to protect and/or maintain the essence and sanctity of life may require suicide to insure that protection and/or maintenance of life.

Barth, comparing and contrasting suicide, confirms the fact that "...in the Bible suicide is nowhere explicitly forbidden."[143] He notes the way in which both testaments have presented the "suicides" of Saul, Ahithophel, and Judas. As a contrast, he cites the example of Sampson:

"If the possibility of Sampson has sometimes to be considered, it can be only at the extreme limit when others have first been examined with seriousness and there can be no doubt whatever that this is the will of God and is therefore to be adopted;" but "As seen by the Bible, he (Sampson) was certainly not a suicide."[144]

In contrast to these biblical examples, Barth notes that there are cases, which we might consider more typical of suicide, where the individual "...regards his (sic) being as an obvious failure, or an intolerable burden, or perhaps for no particular reason as valueless...

---

143 Ibid., p. 408. See also Clemons, J.T.: *What Does the Bible Say About Suicide?*(Nashville: Parthenon Press, 1990), p.10, where the definition of suicide is discussed. Clemons prefers: "Suicide is the choice and the successful completion of the act to end one's life regardless of motive, circumstance, or method." For a more extensive treatment of the definition of suicide see Shneidman, E.: *Definition of Suicide* (New York: John Wiley and Sons, 1985).

144 Ibid. p. 411.

"[145] For Barth this kind of suicide, where God's help is not sought, is a sin, representing self-murder.

This extreme of wanting to die, because of depression or other psychological factors, is in contrast, of course, to the opposite extreme of wanting to live at all costs. Barth makes a telling and critical statement about the irrational desire to prolong one's life: "Wanting to live at all costs can then be only elemental, sinful and rebellious desire."[146] It is clear to Barth that these latter individuals have not "sought" or "listened" to God and are no different from those who arbitrarily end their life. And these typical suicides often occur in isolation, but, concerning the exceptional suicide, Barth wants to make it very clear that none of this occurs in a vacuum. Therefore, such a decision can, in no case, be made in isolation. The human being is never alone: "The fact is that we belong to God, and therefore all the angels of God are on our side, and there is for us inexhaustible, illimitable and unfailing forgiveness, help and hope!"[147]

It is important to note that critics or detractors of Barth's theology and ethics often point to the apparent irrationalism of a "...divine command (that) comes like a thunderbolt out of heaven, brooking no questioning, displacing all thinking."[148] But Barth answers his critics in CDIII/4 under the "Problem of Special Ethics" where he explains that:

"...this does not amount in practice to a direction to let oneself be governed from moment to moment and situation to situation by a kind of direct and particular

---

145   Ibid. p. 403. Noting the extreme mental states that may lead to suicide, Barth observes: "We must remember that the man (sic) who toys with the thought of self-destruction is always in some way in the darkness of affliction (p. 406)."

146   Ibid. p. 401.

147   Ibid. pp. 407-408.

148   Biggar, N, in Webster, J.: p. 215.

divine inspiration and guidance, and to prepare oneself, to make and keep oneself fit and ready, for the reception of such guidance, perhaps by 'quiet times' or similar exercises." He adds: "...while man's (sic) situation is such that step by step he confronts the command of God and has to act in responsibility to it, he himself has to determine what the contents of this command are and therefore how he must act, so that like Goethe's mule he has to find his own way in the mist."[149]

In respecting and obeying the command of God, humankind, then, exemplifies what Barth describes as a multifold covenantal relationship between God and the created order. Indeed, in refuting the charge of monism[150], Barth describes at great length the four-fold nature of the human being's responsibility "in freedom" before God as a creature in God's created order.[151] This four-fold responsibility (Freedom before God, Freedom in Fellowship, Freedom for Life and Freedom in Limitation) frames Barth's social ethic thus, includes the pertinent presentation of the *ultima ratio*.

---

149   Barth, K.: p. 15.
150   See Fletcher, D.B.: "Monism," *Evangelical Dictionary of theology*, Elwell, W.A., Editor (Grand Rapids: Baker Book House, 1984).
151   Barth, K., pp. 47-685. We can not present very much of this extensive analysis of the human's responsibilities before God, but on p. 565, Barth opines that this human is "...under obligation to affirm his (sic) own life and that of others with the special intention indicated by the 'limit' of 'time' and 'vocation' and 'honour,'" and "...we shall then go on to consider the sanctification and obedience of man within it in its first and most important aspect, namely, as the commanded apprehension of existence as a unique opportunity."

To capsule: in extreme cases—most of them seriously ill patients whom Barth describe as at the "frontier of life"— we see where he may make an exception for US, but not AD. These unusual cases would be equivalent to Fried's idea of the "catastrophic" in which the usual moral values of right and wrong do not apply. Similarly, we have cited Paul Ramsey's two qualifications to his (only) caring for the dying: (1) when a patient is "irretrievably inaccessible to human care" and (2) a long death where it is "medically impossible to keep severe pain at bay."[152] Other observers of life in extremis have raised similar qualifications. The ethicist, William F. May, frequently argues against legalizing euthanasia, but he could see where he might kill for mercy's sake "...when the patient is irreversibly beyond human care, terminal and in extreme and unabatable pain."[153]

Therefore, in the following section, again based on the theology of Karl Barth, we see where David Clough would go further than Barth, giving theological justification not only for US, but also for AD. At the same time, he will show us where Christian attitudes toward suffering can go wrong and what is required to right those attitudes. Clough does not explicitly give us notice that there may be serious legal consequences to our actions, but we get such a notice by implication.

4.3. CHRISTIANS AT THE FRONTIER
OF LIFE AND IN HARM'S WAY

Dr. David Clough, from the Department of Religious Studies at Yale University (at last contact Clough was at the University of Durham, Durham, England), has written a challenging article applying the theology of Karl Barth to "End-of-Life Decisions in a Medical

---

152   Ramsey, P.: pp. 161-162.
153   May, W.F.: *The Christian Century*, May 2, 2001.

Context."[154] The basis for the article, and the essence of Clough's argument, is that one can take Barth's trinitarian ethic—the ethic of creation, reconciliation and redemption—and apply it to this question of extreme terminal suffering requiring difficult medical and ethical decisions.

The "ethic" of creation demands respect and protection for life, a free and gracious gift from God, but that demand does not make life an "absolute good." Thus, even though life is finite and dispensable in that sense, the ethic does not allow us to "...dispose of (life) as we chose."[155] But,—and this is the more specific thrust of Clough's argument—"there may be times in which respecting life as God's gift means accepting its ending, or even initiating its destruction."[156]

Under the section on reconciliation, the pertinent points are: (1) God is always with us, therefore, we are never alone; (2) we stand before God as irresolute sinners seeking redemption and reconciliation and (3) we experience God's unconditional, unremitting love as "confirmation" rather than "judgment" on our lives. Therefore, in consideration of this latter experience, we avoid "endemic self-preoccupation," which would result in our sin becoming idolatry. With a proper sense and attitude fueled by the mercy and love of God, an illness will not become an intrusion into our lives, but a "suffering" to be tolerated and overcome. However, if that illness becomes terminal and cannot be overcome, it can easily bring despair, loss of faith and hope, and the thoughts of death as the only comfort. It is easy to see that these persons may seek suicide or AD, but for the wrong reasons. Clough notes: "Persons in this state stand in dire need of repentance." Therefore, turning around and getting

---

154   Clough, D.: "A Theological Framework for End-of-Life Decisions in a Medical Context," Department of Religious Studies, Yale University, New Haven, 1999.
155   Ibid.
156   Ibid.

"right" with God, seeking God's assurances, often requiring pastoral care, may reverse the despair that hinders appropriate, therefore ethical, end-of-life decisions.

The third part of this ethic, redemption, requires that we live a life worthy of God's call, including witnessing to the pagan world. We are also called to speak out on issues that confront and shape our community, including the issue of US and AD. In this setting, persons may discern the limits of that "life worthy of God's call" and, in good faith, seek an early death. This calling, involvement, and discernment may mean that we have to make a decision about AD and face the possible consequences of an illegal act. For example, in Michigan and Georgia, any form of AD is murder. Thus, for Clough and others, AD should remain illegal so as to not reach the "slippery slope" that may result in the killing of incompetent patients or the suicide of a young person with decades of life to live.

Clough concludes that there are times at the end of life when a patient may be beyond any means to prevent her suffering, and in consultation with family and the clergy, chooses to end her life. Even beyond this, these exceptional cases possibly require euthanasia and Clough writes that it may be a Christian's duty to carry out this killing. Here, allowing for euthanasia to be committed by a Christian, goes beyond what Barth would countenance. Clough presents a philosophical, theological and legal conundrum: since PAS remains illegal (or without legal support) in all but two states and since euthanasia is illegal in all states, the Christian who participates in AD may be charged with murder.

Certainly, this piece speaks to a timely topic and exhibits a conscientious, well-reasoned and sincere effort to be a clear and concise voice on behalf of AD. We have to remind ourselves, as Barth does, that these are truly exceptional cases and extremely rare in their occurrence. However, Clough claims that the Christian may be "called" to assist in the suicide of a friend or loved one; and, Clough would see a Christian "duty" to perform a mercy killing (AD) in some extreme cases, realizing that by either action the person may face serious legal consequences. Furthermore, if the Christian "hears" the command of God to assist in, or cause the death of, a hospitalized patient, then the act may become even more difficult, if not impossible, to perform.

Unfortunately, Clough, does not address the questions concerning violence that we have raised through the voices of Yoder, Hays and Hauerwas. Philosophically, one can argue that a mercy killing connotes compassion rather than violence—or the sincere sense of compassion simply overrides the violence enacted. Here, again, the argument that the absolute command of God trumps the ethical norm resounds throughout Clough's thesis.

David Clough, or anyone who argues in favor of AD, should be called to answer the "challenge" put forth by Stanley Hauerwas and Richard Bondi in an essay entitled, "Memory, Community, and the Reasons for Living: Reflections on Suicide and Euthanasia."[157] Their arguments, from the perspective of life as a gift from God, are based on two important concepts among others: (1) the appropriate use of memory that would never deny the future and (2) the inextricable relationship between the Christian and her community. The authors would readily admit that this community is required to discern the tension between the reasons to live and those rare cases in which there are compelling reasons to die, i.e., martyrdom. But, for these Christian scholars, the "usual" notions of suicide and euthanasia are "…incompatible with and subversive of some fundamental elements of the Christian story."[158] For "…it is fundamental to the Christian

---

157　From Berkman, J. and Cartwright, M., Editors: *The Hauerwas Reader: Stanley Hauerwas* (Durham: Duke University Press, 2001), pp. 577-595.

158　Ibid. p. 578.

manner that our lives are formed in terms not of what we will do with them, but of what God will do with our lives, both in our living and our dying."[159] Hauerwas and Bondi admit two things: (1) there are cases of euthanasia that do not "…carry the moral weight normally associated with the judgment implied in the notion of euthanasia," and (2) their relatively uncompromising stance would "…result in some tragic circumstances," but "…that is what the moral life is all about."[160]

I would make a few observations on the Hauerwas and Bondi essay that may broaden the basis for the argument concerning the Christian's response to or for AD. Firstly, the authors do not specifically address AD in the context of the terminal patient for which palliative/hospice has failed; secondly, I can envision the situation in which dying has been prolonged to such an extent that the patient's Christian community, in consensus, desires that the patient be relieved of her suffering; and lastly, Hauerwas and Bondi did not specifically address the tension that may, or should, occur concerning the impending violence of assisted death versus the violence of allowing the patient to suffer more than she can endure. Finally, we should note that Hauerwas and Bondi's stance is an expansion on the idea that AD is incompatible with the apostolic witness of Jesus Christ or the Gospel, strictly applied. With this witness in mind, we turn to a more nuanced discussion of palliative care.

---

159   Ibid. p. 587.
160   Ibid. p. 595.

CHAPTER FIVE

OTHER VOICES: THE ESSENTIAL FEATURES OF TERMINAL CARE

In the care of a dying loved one, the Christian has to discern what "terminal care" entails. What exactly is it? Where does it happen—in the hospital, in a hospice unit, in a nursing home, or at home with family? Does private or public health insurance cover this service? How much of the care is the Christian able to perform?

In terms of exactly what "terminal care" is and where it happens, we often hear the more specific terms "palliative care" and "hospice" used together or interchangeably. Medically, as we shall see, they may be used together, but they are not interchangeable. They are different, as the caring family member soon discerns. What is the difference and is that important? Yes, the difference between palliative and hospice care, though they are intimately related, is important. As I see it, palliative care can stand alone in the hospital or it can be the essential part of, and under the umbrella, of hospice. The dictionary makes a clear distinction between the two: "palliative," a derivative of "to palliate," means "…serving to relieve or lessen without curing."[161] We already have an example of palliative care when, in chapter two, we elaborated on Paul Ramsey's view of traditional medical ethics as it morphed into "comfort care" or (only) caring for the dying. The definition of hospice helps us understand what I mean by palliative care being under the "umbrella" of hospice. Under a "medical" definition, hospice is (a) "a healthcare facility for the terminally ill that emphasizes pain control and emotional support for the patient and family, typically refraining from taking extraordinary measures to prolong life" and (b) "may also be a similar program of care and support for the terminally ill at home."[162] As to which came first is a moot point, because they are now seen as parallel, closely related and interdependent movements.

And briefly, according to Timothy Quill below, the reimbursement for these services, whether they are covered by private or public health insurance plans, remains problematic (problematic or not, this situation is likely to improve). In answer to our final question, the family care-giver is allowed to perform as much of the terminal care as they feel they can competently handle, even without professional supervision.

As evidence of the evolution of this view of terminal care, we now comment on the essential nature of "palliative and/or hospice care" for the dying. (Terminal care for the dying patient, from a clinician's perspective, allows for these terms to be used interchangeably.) Daniel P. Sulmasy, O.F.M, M.D., Ph.D., has, in varied formats and in some detail, espoused his firm conviction that palliative or hospice care, done right, is characterized by the following: (1) there is "appropriate treatment abatement;" (2) the patient and all involved in her care are imbued with the reality of "non-abandonment;" (3) there is appropriate "symptom control;" (4) "hospice and/or palliative care"

---

161   The Random House Dictionary of the English Language, Random House, New York (1987)

162   Ibid.

has been instituted and (5) the patient retains her "dignity—the healing of the dying."[163]

Sulmasy went so far as to say that no patient under his care, no matter the circumstances, has ever asked for assistance in dying. Even so, not every clinician (or any healthcare worker for that matter) has had such success in care at the end of life. As there is uneven or unequal care for the terminally ill, the limitations and what can be done for them are spelled out as follows:

"When one tries to achieve these goals (on providing appropriate care at the end of life) in the real world, one is brought face to face with institutional limitations, human foibles, problems giving care in teams, and challenges of cultural diversity, among other things. Dying, even with the best possible care, can be messy and difficult. Yet, despite these difficulties, much can be done to make dying more comfortable and more humane, and much is done, every day, by patients, family members, and dedicated hospice and palliative care workers."[164]

What, then, is required of the family and other healthcare providers in order for the terminal patient to live out her last hours, days or weeks—rarely months—in as much comfort as possible? In other words, what are the goals that should be set in order that such a patient dies well and does not require any potentially violent intervention? David Roy summarizes these goals under the slogan, "Dying with Dignity":

163 Sulmasy, D.P.: "Physician-Assisted Suicide: A Clinician's Perspective," Kennedy Institute of Ethics Intensive Bioethics Course (June 17, 1997). That same year Sulmasy and Lynn, J., published an article, "End-of-Life Care" in *JAMA* 277 (1997): 1854-55.
164 Barnard, D., et al: *Crossing Over: Narratives of Palliative Care* (New York: Oxford University Press, 2000), p. 1.

"Dying without a frantic technical fuss and bother to squeeze out a few more moments or hours of biological life, when the important thing is to live out one's last moments as fully, consciously, and courageously as possible;

Dying without that twisting, racking pain that totally ties up one's consciousness and leaves one free for nothing and for no one else;

Dying in surroundings that are worthy of a human being who is about to live what should be her 'finest hour.' The environment of a dying patient should clearly say: the technical drama of medicine has receded to the background to give way to the central human drama of a unique human being 'wrestling with his (sic) God;'

Dying in the presence of people who know how to drop the professional role mask and relate to others simply and richly as a human being."[165]

What Sulmasy and Roy are saying is that palliative and/or hospice care—an evolved state of Ramsey's "(only) care for the dying"—at the end of life has been shown, in the vast majority of cases, to be effective and adequate enough to forestall any consideration of suicide or AD.[166] Other more recent voices below confirm the advances in palliative and/or hospice care across a wide range of healthcare facilities and programs. They report on the specific medical advances in the "last resort" options for the patient in extremis at the end of life.

---

165   Ibid., p.3. See full reference on page 16 of the *Crossing Over...*text above.

166   See Dickinson, G.E., et al, "U.K. Physicians' Attitudes Toward Active Voluntary Euthanasia and PAS," *Death Studies* 26 (July-August 2002): 488.

CHAPTER SIX

OTHER VOICES: MEDICAL ADVANCES IN "LAST RESORT" OPTIONS

In 2008 the Hastings Center published a series of essays on, "Choosing Death: Should Medicine's Last 'Last Resort' be Legal?"[167] In lieu of these essays, the question that we will consider is whether or not the current state of medical care can successfully address intractable patient suffering without resorting to PAS and its legalization. Timothy Quill, MD, in considerable detail, outlines the current state of terminal care:

> "Several things are clear: (1) Palliative care and hospice have improved in terms of access and delivery, and they remain the standards of care for addressing the suffering of seriously ill patients. (2) Despite state-of-the-art palliative measures, there will remain a relatively small number of patients whose suffering is insufficiently relieved. (3) Several 'last resort' options, including aggressive pain management, forgoing life-sustaining therapies, voluntarily stopping

---

167   *HCR* 38 (September-October 2008): 17-32.

eating and drinking, and sedation to unconsciousness to relieve otherwise intractable suffering, could address many of these cases."[168]

Despite the recent advances in terminal care,[169] Quill notes that this care has been slow to advance into the outpatient and home settings, and, thus, there remain "...gaps between need and availability..."[170] Clearly, to Quill, we face "serious challenges" in these difficult cases. There are still not enough "skilled" palliative care clinicians to meet the needs of dying patients and "...reimbursement for palliative care services...remains problematic."[171] Fortunately, for those in need of terminal care, Quill states that:

> "Access to palliative care is facilitated by the proliferation of hospice programs. Hospice has expanded considerably in the last ten years, primarily in two domains: the conclusion of terminal ill patients with diseases other than cancer—

---

168   Quill, T.E., p. 17. I need not belabor the point, but the reader should be reminded of the case of "Diane," a patient of Dr. Quill's suffering from leukemia for whom he prescribed barbiturates to allow her to take her own life. Dr. Harmon Smith, based on the moral foundation of traditional Western medicine and the God-given value of human life, finds Quill's rationale for assisting in Diane's death "deeply" problematic and concludes: "This means, in part, that in the exceptional case (see discussion of Karl Barth's *Ultima Ratio)* there may be moral warrant for an appropriate self-sacrifice of one's own life, but it also means that these moral warrants do not extend to the permissibility, much less the duty, to sacrifice the life of another (see *Where Two or Three are Gathered,* p. 202.)"

169   Ibid. "Almost all major medical centers now have inpatient palliative care consultation services, and similar services are spreading into community hospitals."

170   Ibid.

171   Ibid. "... palliative care seems to have passed the 'tipping point' as a field: most patients and families can find the treatments that they need regardless of their stage of disease (pp. 17-18)."

congestive heart failure, dementia, and chronic lung disease, for example—and the ability to supplement the palliative aspects of care for terminally ill patients who reside in skilled nursing homes."[172]

Before this advance in hospice programs, the following restrictions handicapped this terminal care: (1) the attending physician had to "certify" that the patient had no more than six months to live. Traditionally, almost all of these were cancer patients and predicting how long they had to live was fraught with significant error. Thus, the inclusion of patients with other diseases and the easing of the restriction on the length of time to die greatly expanded the scope of hospice; and (2) except for those few programs that have started "bridge" therapy (carry over of some specific therapies from the previous institution in order to maintain stability and comfort for the patient), a dying person could be admitted to hospice only if her definitive treatment was stopped.[173] Thus, because of these prior restrictions, the uneven distribution of hospice care, and other, generally non-medical, reasons, a significant number of patients who die in the United States have not had access to hospice.[174]

We have to consider, then, the "last resort" options for patients who continue to suffer in spite of palliative or hospice care. As we have noted, Quill considers four such options for these patients: the first two options—aggressive pain and symptom management and the forgoing or cessation of life support therapy—are generally not controversial if the patient, or her advocate, understands and consents to either or both of these options.[175] Furthermore, there are legal precedents that support the institution of these two options.

---

172   Ibid., p. 18.
173   Ibid.
174   Ibid.
175   Ibid.

However, the last two options have been, up to this point in time, controversial from a moral or legal standpoint.[176] The third "last resort" option, "voluntarily stopping eating and drinking," called VSED, "...is an informed decision to stop food and fluids in an effort to hasten death and escape suffering."[177] There are those who argue, primarily on a religious basis, than it is unethical to stop vital nourishment, particularly fluids. To them this is an unnecessary, inhumane and non-medical addition to the suffering that a patient is already experiencing. This option—though supported by the attending physician, patient, family members and even some clergy—is still seen by some as suicide or euthanasia, depending on the presence or absence of informed consent.

The final medical option, palliative sedation to unconsciousness (PSU), is an extremely serious decision to render the patient unconscious only in the context of severe, intractable suffering—often with no pain relief—and imminent death.[178] Other life-sustaining measures such as food and fluids are stopped at the same time. This option is used only in these rare and exceptional cases where death is near and the patient is experiencing extreme irreversible suffering, "...but as one gets further away from these circumstances, agreement about its permissibility falls off sharply."[179] And so, below, we seek further understanding about sedation at the end of life.

Margaret P. Battin, professor of philosophy at the University of Utah, has written an essay on "terminal sedation" (equivalent to Quill's PSU) that explores this "last resort" as it compares to

---

176   Ibid., p. 19. "While clearly more morally complex and less settled than the first two options, these (last two) options seem to generate less legal and ethical controversy than physician-assisted death..."
177   Ibid.
178   Ibid.
179   Ibid.

physician-assisted death (PAD).[180] First of all, she observes that terminal sedation is not to be touted as the sole option in extreme suffering at the end of life. Secondly, she analyzes the "irreconcilable" pros and cons of PAD and concludes, "In short, it's autonomy and mercy on the one side (pro) and sanctity of life and/or physical abuse (violence) on the other (con)."[181] Thirdly, she forcefully shared her concern to those who proposed terminal sedation as a compromise to the conflict over PAD. Only by strict guidelines and transparency in front of the patient can terminal sedation be such a compromise. Fourthly, often because of the inability to relieve severe pain, a patient cannot exercise her autonomy and give rational consent for terminal sedation. Battin makes it clear: "…but if pain is severe enough, reflective, unimpaired consent may no longer be possible."[182] Furthermore, even if the consent is secured, the intent of terminal sedation is often obscured—"Terminal sedation may end pain, but it also ends life."[183] Relief of pain, then, is the only "intended" when terminal sedation is offered as a last resort. Fifthly, all the negatives to the contrary, "terminal sedation," done right, can be an effective way to end suffering and sometimes, if planned, to bring about a merciful and peaceful death. "It may be perceived as less final than PAD: some forms of palliative sedation involve raising the level of consciousness periodically—for example, once a day—to see if the patient is still suffering."[184]

Finally, Battin notes that the Supreme Court (1997), using the term "terminal sedation," and the AMA Council on Ethical and Judicial Affairs (2008), using the term "palliative sedation," both, based on

---

180   Battin, M.P.: "*Terminal Sedation: Pulling the Sheet over Our Eyes*" HCR 38, no. 5 (2008): 27-30. I'm not sure why she uses the term, "physician-assisted death," but she is restricting the "enabler" to be a physician.

181   Ibid., p. 27

182   Ibid.

183   Ibid.

184   Ibid., p. 29

the physician's intent with double-effect reasoning, attempted to made a clear distinction between terminal or palliative sedation and euthanasia.[185] What is not clear—in the rather loose use of the terms "terminal" versus "palliative" sedation— is the level of consciousness that is achieved. Quill's use of PSU is unequivocal. The degree of the relief of pain, as the critical determining factor in what you set out to achieve, is problematic. Furthermore, the terms in use relative to terminal sedation have to be clearly defined and agreed upon. If the relief of pain requires PSU, then that has to be clearly stated to, and understood by, the patient. Battin states: "What is astonishing is the AMA's attempt to try to differentiate between different sorts of clinical intentions on the basis of observed practice, when it is simply not possible— nor morally defensible—to draw this false line between them."[186]

Thus, Battin and Quill both recognize the need for guidelines that would control the use of terminal sedation and lessen the need to differentiate "clinical intentions." Battin elaborates on the problem:

> "the implausible effort to draw a completely bright line between continuous terminal sedation and euthanasia makes the practice of terminal sedation both more dangerous and more dishonest than it should be---and makes what can be a decent and humane practice morally problematic."[187]

In response to "letters" to her discussion of "terminal sedation" in the Hastings Center Report, and to further clarify her stance on the "morally problematic" possibility of this option, Battin states:

---

185   Ibid.
186   Ibid., p. 30. She concludes: "There is no reason that terminal sedation should not be recognized as an option, but there are excellent reasons why it should not be seen as the *only* option---or even the best option---for easing a bad death."
187   Ibid.

"It is simply not morally defensible to keep a competent, potentially autonomous patient from being able to choose between pain and death, though this is the effect that resorting to terminal sedation—especially if innocuously packaged as 'palliative sedation' and sold only as relief of pain—may often have."[188]

These legitimate and serious concerns by Dr. Battin were "voiced" in 2008. Nearly two years later, Jeffrey T. Berger addressed the then current guidelines for the use of palliative sedation, emphasizing its use to unconsciousness (PSU), noting that it is "...reserved for cases (of terminally ill patients) in which severe symptoms persist despite intensive interdisciplinary efforts to find a tolerable palliative treatment that does not effect the patient's level of consciousness."[189] Berger exhibited more concern for the side effects of high does of narcotics than he did for the adverse effect of the pain on the patient's ability to make decisions. Up until 2007 the "authoritative guidelines" for PSU were as follows: 1) patient has a terminal condition; 2) the symptoms are intolerable and refractory; 3) the expected survival is no more than "hours to days," but other authorities varied in their response (for example, the Royal Dutch Medical Association gave "one to two weeks") and 4) permissible for existential suffering (only 3 of 7 "consensus panels" said "yes").[190]

Berger's biggest concern is the effect of PSU on the patient's survival: since food and water are stopped at the same time as PSU, then it is possible that dehydration will result in the death of the patient rather than the disease process itself. Therefore he proposes

---

188   From "Margaret Battin replies" to a letter to the editor in *HCR* 39 (March-April 2009): 8.

189   Berger, J.T.: "Rethinking Guidelines for the Use of Palliative Sedation," *HCR* 40, no. 3 (2010): 33.

190   Ibid.

the following changes in the guidelines: 1) the time to death from disease is less than or equal to time to death from PSU-induced dehydration; 2) there is informed consent from patient or surrogate and 3) there is severe existential suffering for which all available and reasonably effective treatments are unacceptable to the patient.[191] Furthermore, if PSU is not expected to shorten survival, Berger would lift "... the requirements of having refractory symptoms and a survival time of hours to days."[192]

———————————

In summary, then, we have addressed medical advances in "last resort" options for patients experiencing unremitting suffering at the end-of-life. We have asked if these options are ethical and whether or not PAS as the last "last resort" should be legalized. T. E. Quill argues that there are rare patients who do not respond to palliative and/or hospice care and, therefore, should have the final option to be aided in taking their own life. In addition, then, to Oregon and Washington, he would advocate for the legalization of PAS in all states.

Daniel Callahan, also writing from the Hastings Center, recognizes and points out the risk for involuntary euthanasia that such action would incur when the patient is not competent to make such a decision. Give Quill credit, he cited the advances that have been make in the care of the terminally ill patient, especially in terms of palliative and hospice care, and, thus, the pressure to go beyond that care has been lessened considerably.

We also reviewed one of the very serious and controversial last medical options known as PSU, palliative sedation to unconsciousness, and the equally serious, and to some unethical and "non-medical," option of VSED, voluntarily stopping of eating and drinking. And we

191   Ibid., p. 36.
192   Ibid.

noted that VSED is also part of the PSU option, so there is a double whammy. Two additional scholars, Battin and Berger, commented on the vicissitudes of PSU and the need for further evaluation of the terminal therapy and the criteria for its use. Battin was rightfully concerned about the affect of pain on the patient's ability to make a rational decision concerning the PSU option and Berger was equally concerned about the VSED portion of PSU causing the patient to die prematurely from dehydration. I am not sure that Berger adequately addressed Battin's concerns about the effect of pain on the informed consent that is required for PSU. He was actually more concerned about the side effects of narcotics used to treat the pain. The consent by a surrogate—a potential ethical problem—is not mentioned by either author, but both admit that PSU can be a moral minefield and that there is much more to be "elucidated."[193]

---

193   Ibid., p. 37. Berger ends with a statement about patients whose survival time is likely to be shortened: then PSU becomes "...an outlier medical practice, its moral relationship to active euthanasia is not well defined, and the extent of its ethical complexities has not been fully elucidated."

CHAPTER SEVEN

WHEN DEATH IS NEAR, DOES HOPE ABIDE?

The word, "hope," connotes all things positive and, thus, one of the simplest definitions of hope is: "optimistic expectations."[194] Adrienne M. Martin, a philosopher and ethicist at the University of Pennsylvania, writes about the exploitation of hope in patients considering "unlikely" cures. In consideration of this exploitation, she expands on the above definition of "hope" by adding three "points": (1) "Hope for an outcome involves the *desire* for it"; (2) "Hope involves *imaginative engagement* with the desired outcome, such as prayer, mental imaging, or fantasizing"; and (3) "Emotions, including hope, play a *framing role* in relation to our uptake, interpretation, and deliberative use of information."[195] These points give "hope" a complexity beyond a simple positive attitude. It involves "wanting," "imagining," and "evaluating" the thing hoped for. Hope, as an human trait, can be abused by well-intentioned medical personnel and family.

---

194   *The Random House Dictionary of the English Language.*
195   From "Hope and Exploitation," *HCR* 38 (September-October 2008): 49-55.

Therefore, we have to be careful when we say, "never give up hope," for, in medicine, we are constrained, careful not to raise false hopes based on the prospect of a questionable therapy. This is particularly true when the patient is terminal and the prospects of improving her quality of life are virtually nil. On the other hand, in the general sense of the human existential condition, we have to be careful not to douse the flame of hope that "springs eternal in the human breast."[196] For those of us in the Christian faith, there is hope for eternal life, based on the "...blood and righteousness of Jesus Christ." This hope is essentially synonymous with the belief or faith that God is the Lord of life and death, now and eternal, and into whose "hands" we will fall.[197]

(Aside from, or beyond this Christian characteristic of remaining hopeful, one wonders whether hope is present at birth or is it a learned, experienced trait. Should we question whether or not hope is inborn and therefore close to an instinct? It seems to me that hope is not in the same category as the five senses, which, short of disease, accident or old age, are not lost. Whatever the origin or essence of hope, and aside from the religious viewpoint, we instinctively guard against, are sensitive to, losing hope.)

Whatever the case, we are acutely aware of the need for the sick person to maintain an realistic hopeful attitude, whether living and getting well or dying and facing death. We also know that a positive attitude, especially in prayer, contributes to the process of healing. No matter the state of health or disease, the more the patient— honestly accepting the knowledge of her condition—expresses her hopes and fears, the more she can approach a peaceful state. In some cases, approaching a peaceful state may not be possible—whether the patient is suffering severe unremitting pain, depression, and/or

---

196   Alexander Pope.

197   See 1Cor 13:13 which reads, "And now faith, hope and love abide, these three; and the greatest of these is love." (NRSV)

existential angst—unless such a state is induced with medication (palliative sedation).

Assurances of loving care by the steadfast presence of family, friends and medical staff may keep the patient realistically hopeful when she is consciously aware of her surroundings. We have implied that it is certainly disingenuous on the part of a physician to offer the dying patient "one last hope," a new drug, or an invasive procedure to forestall death one last time. This attitude that "death is the enemy" was at one time pervasive, but slowly this attitude is dying. Similarly, it has been long debated about how much the patient should know of her condition, but honesty, not secrecy, has been shown to be the best policy.

However, there are times, in contrast to remaining hopeful, when no matter what is said or not said, the patient "suffers" from the fear of dying. Here the presence of clergy can fill a void by helping the patient realize that another life is beginning and there is hope rather than fear in dying. And so, when the patient is ready to die and the family is in agreement, all life support may be removed and with control of pain the patient may die in peace. She may be "letting go," but she is not "giving up hope in the future." No doubt some deaths are hard and "messy," but it is extremely rare that a patient cannot be kept comfortable with no fear of losing her life.

This whole discussion on whether hope abides when death is near is about the psychological, philosophical and theological basis for understanding the suffering patient at the end of life and how she sees dying and death. In summary, there are few better quotes about "hope" than from Plato's *Apology*:

> "If it is not possible for modern men (sic), when the 'lone hope' is gone, to believe that this is not the end of hope, perhaps we might share the conviction of Socrates, who

said, 'Now it is time that we were going, I to die and you to live, but which of us has the happier prospect, is unknown to anyone but God.' That outlook, too, might save men and doctors today from the triumphalist temptation to slash and suture our way to eternal life."[198]

---

198   Ramsey, P., p. 238.

CHAPTER EIGHT

CONCLUSION: ANSWERS TO
THE QUESTION RAISED

Against the question raised, "Are there end-of-life situations where the usual healthcare fails, the universal prohibition against killing is suspended, and suicide (US) or assisted death (AD) become the Christian's response to relieve her own or another person's suffering?" we begin with pertinent comments decrying the institution of PAS (which, we have noted, falls under AD). Dr. D. P. Sulmasy, a physician and Ph.D. ethicist, believes that PAS is "bad medicine," "bad morals," and "bad public policy." He reasons that PAS is based on ill-conceived notions that it is "therapeutic" (bad medicine), is based on an "atomistic[199] conception of human

---

199   The Random House Dictionary of the English Language: Atomism: "the theory that minute, discrete, finite, and indivisible elements are the ultimate constituents of all matter." See also de la Chaumiere, p. 88-89, where, according to this theory, "...the origins of the cosmos and the subsequent ongoing events are the result of blind chance," but "nature for Plato is not the result of atoms moving mechanistically through empty space, a product of chance, but rather is the artistic expression of a benevolent intelligence in a universe that at its foundations is purposeful, moral, and rational."

beings" (bad morals), and is based on the belief that the "legal safeguards are enforceable" (bad public policy).[200] Furthermore, Sulmasy steadfastly holds that there can be prevention of terminal "existential angst" and that, with successful hope-imbued palliative care, PAS is not an issue for consideration. Beyond what Sulmasy contends, we have commented on how advances in the medical care of the sick and dying, including the morally sensitive palliative sedation, are continuing to minimize the "need" for consideration of PAS. In addition to this concerned physician, there are Christian theologians such as with Hauerwas and Bondi who contend that life is a gift from God and, therefore, sacred or holy. Thus, these "euthanasiac" acts are incompatible with the Christian faith, the Christian's reverence for life through memory and her inviolate communion with the Christian community. Hauerwas and Bondi admit that there may be extreme cases of suffering that give one pause, but "that such tragedies are part of the moral life."

Furthermore, Hauerwas and Hays agree with Yoder that Jesus is the ultimate model for a life of nonviolent resistance, booking no violent confrontation with any aspect of the secular world. Those, then, who espouse the apostolic witness of Jesus Christ and the Gospel, strictly applied, live a life of non-violence and would, therefore, strongly oppose any form of suicide or assisted death including PAS. Therefore, based on these Christian witnesses, the answer to our question is a *"qualified no."* The answer is qualified because, in this context, there are rare exceptions to the prohibition against killing: (1) morally justified cases of martyrdom and (2) similarly justified cases of suicide in women subjected to brutal physical abuse.

---

200 Sulmasy, D.P.: "Physician-Assisted Suicide: A Clinician's Perspective," Kennedy Institute of Ethics, Georgetown University, Intensive Bioethics Course (June 19, 1997)

In contrast to these views, we have seen that there are other Christian professionals who advocate the "necessity" of suicide or assisted death in extreme and exceptional cases of suffering at the end of life. In particular, the theologian Karl Barth reasons that there are situations at the end of life which may call for unassisted suicide by a Christian person/patient. I cannot categorically say that he is wrong— he starts with the concept of the human being standing "naked" before God, exposing her foibles, vulnerability and hopelessness. Stripped bare and judged in all her weaknesses, she is alone except for the grace of God. Her life, a relative "good," is under the protection and care of God and her fellow humans. However, when that life, subject to a painful terminal disease, becomes too onerous, the protection and care of that life may extend to her self-imposed death. As we have noted, Barth emphasizes that this event does not occur in isolation, but in the presence of the one who receives her, all God's angels, her family, and her caring Christian community.

Many theologians have voiced concerns that Barth's view is irrational, a sudden "thunderbolt" from heaven that dictates action on the part of the discerning Christian. Barth counters that his view of the exceptional case is based on his trinitarian ethic and, cannot be anything but rational. It is based on the deeply held belief that this creating, reconciling, and redemptive God would in his mercy command that a patient in extremis would have her life "protected" by losing it in self-destruction. We have to be clear here: Barth would not countenance any form of imposed death in this setting, except the patient's suicide by her own hand. As we have seen, Dr. Harmon Smith makes a strong point in agreement with Barth's stance that there may be "moral warrants" in such cases for self-imposed death.

But there are those (including Ramsey, Fried, McCormick, Clough and May) who argue, in contrast to Barth and Smith, that there are rare catastrophic, "inhuman" situations that call for a reasoned response to end a patient's life. They argue that these cases are beyond right or wrong and, as I interpret their sentiments, this response would best be described as "mercy killing."

So, again addressing the question that we are wrestling with, based primarily on Barth's Christian witness, the answer has to be a "qualified yes": there may be extremely rare cases where palliative and/or hospice care and other end-of-life options have failed, the proscription against killing is suspended, and, as a command from God, unassisted suicide becomes the Christian's response to relieve her own suffering. Once again, this second answer is also qualified since it does not address the other part of the question: "...relieve another's suffering," which, we have noted above, is euthanasia championed by Clough, also as a command by God. As I have noted with Barth, I can not categorically say that Clough is wrong. But I have serious reservations concerning the consequences of euthanasia—it is not legal in any setting in the United States and it would be difficult to pull off in a hospital setting. We are left with the less-than-perfect two qualified answers to our question concerning decisions made at the end of life—a never ending conundrum that will continue to require analysis and opinion.

CHAPTER NINE

EPILOGUE

Finally, I have thought long and hard about this question concerning decisions at the end of life. I have to conclude that I cannot discern the nuances of scriptural exegesis or philosophical analysis to the extent required for a single, reasoned, and unambiguous response. But—this I know—if I were a dying conscious patient *in extremis*, I would reject suicide (US) or assisted death (AD) as the last option.

Furthermore and firstly, if I am suffering beyond human reason, and if the guidelines are strictly followed, I would readily choose PSU as my last option. And, as part of PSU, I would expect and support the institution of VSED. Secondly, at least once a day, I would also expect to be brought to consciousness to determine my level of pain or discomfort. Thirdly and lastly, I would expect to die "in peace."

Here, as a final comment relative to the above sentiments, I think it would be logical to consider whether *involuntary* stopping of eating and drinking—not part of PSU—is ever warrented or justified, realizing that this action is tantamount to assisted death or euthanasia. I refer the reader back to the first page of the "Introduction," where I presented a personal testimony about the decision my family and I made at the end of my mother's life. Unconscious, she was unable to respond to us, was unable to eat or drink, and, at the end of a long battle with dementia, had no prospects of ever becoming a reasoning person who could recognize herself and others. We stopped all life support, food, and fluids. She was dead in a matter of days.

Is this tantamount to a "mercy killing" and, therefore, involuntary euthanasia? Or, is it simply a medical decision whereby a natural process of death would not be prolonged and the patient would no longer suffer. Personally, I don't see the difference between these two. Is this a classic example of an end-of-life decision caught in the cross hairs of what is right and what is wrong? Or, given the circumstances, does this question push the religious or philosophical envelope to the point that one has to say that this wrong was a right? Speaking only for me, I have no regrets.

BIBLIOGRAPHY

1. Ayer, A.J.: *The Meaning of Life* (New York: Charles Scriber's Sons, 1990), p. 180.

2. Barth, K.: *Church Dogmatics III/4: The Doctrine of Creation*, Bromiley, G.W. and Torrance, T.F., Editors. (Edinburgh: T.&T. Clark, 1961) (By general convention used in the text as "CDIII/4").

3. _____: *Epistle to the Romans*, translated from the sixth edition by Edwyn C. Hoskyns and Geoffrey Cumberlege. (London, New York, Toronto: Oxford University Press, 1950).

4. Barnard, D., Towers, A., Boston, P., and Lambrinidou, Y.: *Crossing Over: Narratives of Palliative Care* (New York: Oxford University Press, 2000).

5. Bascom, P.B. and Tolle, S.W.: "Responding to Requests for Physician-Assisted Suicide," *JAMA* 288 (2002): 91-98. (64 references)

6. Battin, M.P.: "Terminal Sedation: Pulling the Sheet Over Our Eyes," *Hastings Center Report* 38 (September-October 2008): 27-30. (used by convention in text as "*HCR.*")

7. Berger, J. T.: "Rethinking Guidelines for the Use of Palliative Sedation," *HCR* 40, no. 3 (2010): 32-38.

8. Berlinger, N.: "Helping People Out," *HCR* 39 (January-February 2009): last page, unnumbered.

9. Biggar, N.: "Barth's Trinitarian Ethic" in Webster, J., editor: *The Cambridge Companion to Karl Barth* (Cambridge: Cambridge University Press, 2000), pp. 212-227. (Essential reading to get a grasp of Barth's ethics.)

10. Brueggermann, W.: "Biblical Authority," *The Christian Century* (January 3-10, 2001): 14-20.

11. Callahan, D.: "Pursuing a Peaceful Death," *HCR* 23 (July-August, 1993).

12. _____: "Medical Technology and the Human Future: Slippery Slope," *The Christian Century* (September-October, 2002)

13. _____: "Organized Obfuscation: Advocacy for Physician-Assisted Suicide," *HCR* 38 (September-October 2008) (Enlightening comments on euthanasia in the Netherlands)

14. Chochinov, H.M.: "Dignity-Conserving Care—A New Model for Palliative Care," *JAMA* 287 (May 2002): 2253. (69 references)

15. Clemons, J.T., *What does the Bible Say About Suicide?* (Nashville: Parthenon Press, 1990).

16. Clough, D.: "A Theological Framework for End-of-Life Decisions in a Medical Context," Department of Religious Studies, Yale University, New Haven (March 1999).

17. Craddock, F.B.: *Luke: Interpretation* (Louisville: Knoxville Press, 1990).

18. Curry, L., et.al.: "Could Adequate Palliative Care Obviate Assisted Suicide?" *Death Studies* 26 (November 2002): 757-774. (42 references)

19. De la Chaumiere, R.: *What's it all about? A Guide to Life's Basic Questions and Answers* (Sonoma, California: Wisdom House Press, 2004).

20. Dickinson, G.E., et.al.: "U. K. Physicians' Attitudes Toward Active Voluntary Euthanasia and Physician-Assisted Suicide," *Death Studies* 26 (July-August 2002): 479-489.

21. Duntley, M.A.: "Covenantal Ethics and Care for the Dying," *The Christian Century* (December 4, 1991).

22. Editorial Comment: *The Christian Century* 118 (May 2, 2001).

23. Emanuel, E.: "Whose Right to Die?" *The Atlantic Monthly* (March 1997): 73-79.

24. _____: et.al.: "Attitudes and Desires Related to Euthanasia and Physician-Assisted Suicide Among Terminally Ill Patients and Their Caregivers," *JAMA* 284 (November 15, 2000): 2460-2468.

25. Fitzgerald, F.T.: "The Tyranny of Health," *NEJM* 331 (July 21, 1994): 196-198. (Highly recommended read for a redefinition of "health.")

26. Fletcher, D.B.: "Monism," in Elwell, W.A., Editor, *Evangelical Dictionary of Theology* (Grand Rapids: Bake Book House, 1984).

27. Fried, C.: *Right and Wrong* (Cambridge: Cambridge University Press,1978).

28. Franklin, S.: *Encyclopedia of Bioethics*, Vol. 3, Reich, W.T., Editor in Chief. (New York: Simon and Schuster Macmillan,1995), p.1346.

29. Grieb, A.K., "'Time Would Fail Me to Tell...': The Identity of Jesus Christ in Hebrews" in Gaventa, B.R. and Hays, R.B., editors: *Seeking the Identity of Jesus: A Pilgrimage* (Grand Rapids: William B. Eerdmans, 2008), pp. 204, 213.

30. Hall, A.L.: *Kierkegaard and the Treachery of Love* (Cambridge: Cambridge University Press, 2002), pp.54-81.

31. Hays, R.B.: *The Moral Vision of the New Testament* (HarperSanFrancisco, 1996).

32. Hauerwas, S.: *With the Grain of the Universe* (Grand Rapids, Michigan: Brazos Press, a Division of Baker Book House, 2001). (The Gifford Lectures)

33. _____ and Bondi, R.: "Memory, Community, and the Reasons for Living: Reflections on Suicide and Euthanasia" in Berkman, J. and Cartwright, M., Editors, *The Hauerwas Reader: Stanley Hauerwas* (Durham: Duke University Press, 2001), pp. 577-595.

34. _____: *The Peaceable Kingdom* (Notre Dame: University of Notre Dame Press, 1983).

35. _____: "Rational Suicide and Reasons for Living" in *On Moral Medicine* (Grand Rapids: William B. Eerdmans Co.,1998), pp.671-678.

36. Keck, D.: *Forgetting Whose We Are: Alzheimer's Disease and the Love of God* (Nashville: Abingdon Press, 1996).

37. Kempis, T.A.: *The Imitation of Christ* (New York: Hurst and Co. Publishers, no date).

38. Kierkegaard, S.: *Fear and Trembling/Repetition* (Princeton: Princeton University Press, 1983).

39. Kingsolver, B.: *The Poisonwood Bible* (New York: HarperPerennial, 1998).

40. Kliever, L. D.: *Encyclopedia of Bioethics*, Vol. 1, Reich, W. T., Editor in Chief. (New York: Simon and Schuster Mcmillan,1995), p. 511.

41. Lamont, C.: *The Philosophy of Humanism* (New York: Frederick Unger, 1982).

42. Liegner, L.M.: "St. Christopher's Hospice, 1974, Care of the Dying Patient," *JAMA* 234 (1975).

43. Lynn, J. and Sulmasy, D.P.: "End-of-Life Care," *JAMA* 277 (1997): 1854-1855. (The then current state of improving the quality of care at the end of life).

44. Lynn, J.: "Serving Patients Who May Die Soon and their Families: The Role of Hospice and Other Services," *JAMA* 285 (2001): 925-932.

45. Martin, A.M.: "Hope and Exploitation," *HCR* 38 (September-October 2008): 49-55. (Excellent expose on hope as it relates to patient deliberation on an "unlikely" cure.)

46. May, W.F.: Editorial, *The Christian Century* (May 2001).

47. McCormick, R.A.: "Physician-Assisted Suicide: Flight from Compassion," *The Christian Century* (1991): 1132-1134. (This is a "must read")

48. _____: "Ambiguity in Moral Choice," The Pere Marquette Theology Lecture (1973).

49. Meier, D., et.al.: "A National Survey of Physician-Assisted Suicide and Euthanasia in the United States," *NEJM* 338 (1998): 1193-1201. (Definition of PAS/Euthanasia)

50. Metaxas, E.: *Bonhoeffer: Pastor, Martyr, Prophet, Spy* (Nashville: Thomas Nelson, 2010). (Must read to understand Bonhoeffer's role as "spy.")

51. Metzger, R.M. and Coogan, M.D., Editors: *The Oxford Companion to the Bible* (New York and Oxford: Oxford University Press, 1993), pp.43-44.

52. Morreim, E.H.: "Profoundly Diminished Life: The Casualties of Coercion," *HRC* 24 (January-February, 1994).

53. Pelican, J.: *Jesus Through the Centuries* (New Haven: Yale University Press, 1985).

54. Pojman, L.P., Editor: *Life and Death: A Reader in Moral Problem* (Sudbury, Massachusetts: Jones and Bartlett Publishers,1993). (Highly recommended reading: Taylor, R.: "Does Life Have a Meaning?" Part III, Chapter 15, 157-166).

55. Quill, T.E.: "Physician-Assisted Death in the United States: Are the Existing 'Last Resorts' Enough?" *HRC* 38 (2008)

56. Ramsey, P.: *The Patient as Person: Exploration in Medical Ethics* (New Haven: Yale University Press, 1970).

57. Scherer, J.M. and Simon, R.J.: *Euthanasia and the Right to Die: A Comparative View* (Lanham, Maryland: Rowman & Littlefield Publishers, Inc.,1999). (good statistics, extensive notes and extended bibliography).

58. Sulmasy. D.P.: "Physician-Assisted Suicide: A Clinician's Perspective," Kennedy Institute of Ethics, Georgetown University, Intensive Bioethics Course (June 19, 1997).

59. Shneidman, J.: *Definition of Suicide* (New York: John Wiley and Sons, 1985).

60. Shuman, J.: "Constancy: Being Sick and Dying as We Have Lived" from *The Body of Compassion* (Bolder: Westview Press, 1999), pp.134-142.

61. Smith, H.L.: *Where Two or Three are Gathered* (Cleveland: The Pilgrim Press, 1995). (See, in particular, the section on "Christian Reflections on Suffering and Suicide," p. 200.)

62. Steinhauser, K.E., et.al.: "Factors Considered Important at the End of Life by Patients, Physicians, and Other Care Providers," *JAMA* 284 (November 15, 2000).

63. "Near the Cross": *The Hymnal for Worship and Celebration* (Waco Texas: Word Music,1936), p. 385.

64. *The Random House Dictionary of the English Language* (New York: Random House, 1987).

65. *"My Hope Is Built": The United Methodist Hymnal* (Nashville: The United Methodist Publishing House, 1993), p. 368.

66. Vanderpool, H.Y.: *Doctors and the Dying of Patients in American History* in Weir, R.F. (see #67 below)

67. Weir, R.F., Editor: *Physician-Assisted Suicide* (Bloomington and Indianapolis: Indiana University Press, 1997).

68. Wright, N.T.: *Simply Christian: Why Christianity Makes Sense* (New York: HarperOne, 2006).

69. Yoder, J.H.: *The Politics of Jesus* (Grand Rapids: William B. Eerdmans Publishing Company, 1994).

70. _____: *The Priestly Kingdom* (Notre Dame: University of Notre Dame Press, 1984)

GLOSSARY

1. <u>AD</u>: Assisted Death: as it relates to end-of-life care: a medical case in which an "enabler" or helper assists in the death of a patient; includes PAS and PAD (see below).

2. <u>Death</u>: Classic definition: loss of life force with absent heart beat, pulse and respiration; modern definition: brain death with loss of cerebral function or whole brain death with loss of cerebral and brainstem function.

3. <u>DND</u>: Death with Dignity: means different things to different people, but, in simple terms, is most akin to a "peaceful death" or an uncomplicated—not a messy—death; patient has not lost her human characteristic as "dignified;" PAS (see below) statutes in Oregon and Washington were purported to be "death with dignity" citizen initiatives.

4. <u>Diminished life</u>: As it relates to a patient *in extremis*, her life may be "diminished," "less than," or "reduced in value." If life is considered to have "absolute value," then diminishment is a contradiction.

5. <u>Disease</u>: Literally an "ill ease," a state in which an individual has "contracted" a localized or systemic abnormality which underlies an illness or sickness. A "terminal illness" implies an underlying disease which will take the person's life.

6. Euthanasia: Literally a "good death;" the act of "mercy killing;" in wartime, the practice of "gassing" a prisoner. With consent of the "victim" called voluntary; without consent called involuntary; without consent and knowledge, non-voluntary.

7. Last Resort: End-of-life acts when medical options are extremely limited; usually related to palliative or hospice care intended to make the patient as comfortable as possible; some have designated AD as the "last" last resort, indicating that this act is beyond what medical options are available to alleviate terminal suffering.

8. Life: The classis definition from Aristotle, "vitalism," confirms the presence of a vital "force" which gives form and function to the living entity. To Aristotle, life was independent of any external force, but, however, he does admit that human intelligence suggests the "spark" of the divine. Eventually, with evolution, life manifested a connectedness between all living beings and the complicated but predictable stages of development over centuries. The religious definition stated that life was a gift from God exemplified by the incarnation of Jesus Christ.

9. Martyrdom: Choosing death over life because of one's faith or for the sake of others; not considered suicide (see below).

10. Mercy Killing: See euthanasia above.

11. Patient: A person who is ill, sick or diseased and who is under the care of a healthcare provider, usually a physician or someone under her supervision.

12. PAD: Physician-assisted death: a term implying suicide or euthanasia with a physician as "enabler."

13. PAS: Physician-assisted suicide whereby a physician aids an individual in bringing her life to an end; methods have varied, but the standard for Oregon and Washington is the preparation of barbiturate-laced chocolate pudding.

14. PSU: Palliative sedation to unconsciousness: one of the very last resorts, when death is imminent, whereby the patient is rendered unconscious by a sedative. It is not as controversial as AD, but it remains morally problematic and has been touted in some circles as tantamount to euthanasia. There are current guidelines for its use and the emphasis may be relief of pain, but, since there is cessation of food and fluids, dehydration may shorten the life of the patient. One "compassionate" procedure is to lighten up on the sedation to see if the patient is still suffering.

15. Suicide: The deliberate taking of one's own life regardless of motive, circumstance, or method; other terms include self-murder, self-destruction, and self-annihilation.

16. US: Unassisted suicide, see the *ultima ratio* below.

17. *Ultima Ratio*: Literally the "last argument," a term used by Karl Barth concerning the "exceptional case" whereby he reasons that a person or patient may be in such "throes" at the end of life that she is commanded by God to commit US.